THIS ONE'S FOR YOU

AN INSPIRATIONAL JOURNEY THROUGH
ADDICTION, DEATH, AND MEANING

THIS ONE'S FOR YOU

*AN INSPIRATIONAL JOURNEY THROUGH
ADDICTION, DEATH, AND MEANING*

What Others Are Saying About This One's For You

Wow! There is something for everyone in 'This One's For You.' Parents, friends, teachers, and coaches who work with young people, all of us – there are many messages. Facing problems with children and young adults, everyone can appreciate the experience. It is a tough but very worthwhile adventure. A thoughtful look at serious family challenges – with workable solutions offered as well.

Dr. Tom Davis
Retired Men's Basketball Coach
University of Iowa 1986-1999

Golf is a great game enjoyed by many. It is a game that teaches us many of life's lessons: Sportsmanship, honesty, problem solving, patience, respect to name a few. I have known the Johnston family for over 15 years and watched in amazement how Jeff and his family have dealt with the pain and suffering from the loss of a son and brother. They have chosen this tragic moment in their life as an opportunity to educate and help others who may be in a similar situation and used the game of golf as a vehicle to help create awareness. Jeff's book is thought provoking and details the reality of addiction, gives you his perspective and insight, as well as hope for the future."

Larry Gladson
PGA Golf Professional
Elmcrest Country Club

It's a club no one should ever want to join - losing a child to addiction and overdose. Author, father, and businessman Jeff Johnston's decision to write a book and form a foundation to help others will surely be life changing for many. In his darkest hours he somehow found inspiration and a way forward. I highly recommend 'This One's for You'.

Steve Grant, Author of "Don't Forget Me: A Lifeline of Hope for Those Touched by Substance Abuse and Addiction" and founder of Chris and Kelly's HOPE Foundation

As a father, as a professional in the financial services industry, and as someone who has dealt with my own addiction issues, Jeff's message and his personal journey have had a profound impact in my life. His inspiration transcends generations, ideologies, and occupations. I am certain that the positive impact Jeff continues to have in the lives of so many others will keep Seth's memory alive in perpetuity. I have the fortunate privilege of drawing inspiration from many individuals inside the financial advisor community. Jeff, I can't thank you enough for humbly occupying a seat at the pinnacle of that list. #GoodAdvisorsFinishFirst

John Stadtmueller
VP, Regional Wealth Consultant
LPL Financial

Very emotional and passionate love of family. Having lost my dad at 36, and a brother at 33, I understand the grief and shock in losing a family member. I've learned that no matter how much success you attain in life, nothing compares to the two-way love and affection of family & friends. This book has that.

Jeff's book tugs at the heart, reminding us all to hug our kids daily and be there for them always. Even then, tragedy can strike, but in time, together you are better prepared to move forward.

Gary Dolphin, 'Voice of the Hawkeyes'
Iowa Hawkeye Radio Network

This One's For You" is a heartfelt, emotional and reality check of what substance abuse can lead to. It is a true reminder that tragedy can strike anyone at any time. This book is a deeply personal look into how out of grief, purpose is revealed!!

Kenyon Murray
Former Iowa Hawkeyes Basketball Player

My introduction to the AJGA (American Junior Golf Association) was as a sponsor but my love and passion to work with the young men and women of junior golf ultimately led me to where I am today. The AJGA, and specifically Leadership Links, has provided me the opportunity to hear tremendous stories of perseverance and determination. The Johnston's unique journey is one of dedication and ultimately love in the face of unimaginable pain and suffering. The beauty of what they have done has been an inspiration to us all. "This One's For You" will be a tremendous guide for those families battling addiction and substance abuse and a stark reminder that life, like golf, is often unfair and cruel yet ultimately a true test of resolve and character.

Kevin Rinker, Senior VP of
Development in charge of the AJGA Foundation

Jeff has a passion for using his difficult story as a parent to help others with the challenges of family substance use disorder. He strives to remove the stigma that many associate with addiction and helps to connect people to help and resources that can overcome the fear and despair that families feel when seeking answers. His story provides help and hope.

Jeanette Archer-Simons
Executive Director
Area Substance Abuse Council

How the Johnston family coped with the tragic loss of Seth, raising funding for ASAC and awareness to the current opioid epidemic, is truly inspiring. What Ian did on the golf course during his four years of high school golf is unparalleled at Prairie High School, becoming the best player in school history; what Ian and his family have done off the golf course, the work they have done to raise funds for ASAC to help people battling addiction, is even more impressive.

Erik Columbus
Golf Coach
Prairie HS

For Prudence, Ian, Roman, and Brighton

In memory of Seth Carnicle
(1993 – 2016)

To my parents, Dave and Gerry
Thank you for teaching me compassion and that I hold the key to
unlocking my mind.

Introduction

My moment of epiphany came the minute my eyes met his one afternoon in the Fall of 2018. I had just completed a long, emotional day of speaking at Prairie High School in Cedar Rapids, Iowa. It was the second year in a row I had the honor of telling our story to the impressionable, youthful minds of Ms. Powers' Freshman Health classes. While I am always grateful to speak with students about substance abuse and share our story, it does make for an emotional day with many ups and downs.

My Youngest Son Roman & I speaking to Ms. Powers' Health Class

As I was wrapping up, a well-dressed young man, no more than fourteen years old, walked up to me with tears in his eyes. He was visibly shaken. I knew something I said had touched a nerve or moved him deeply. He humbly proceeded to tell me he had been in rehab and could relate to our story, and he was happy to be alive. You see, his parents were alcoholics, it ran in his family, and he became one by the age of fourteen.

I was stunned, fourteen years old. Fourteen! For a brief moment, I stared at him, unable to form words or say much of anything. I was heartbroken yet, at the same time, in complete admiration of his courage to share this personal chapter in his young life. He proceeded to hand me a crumpled piece of paper with his name on it and scribbled in blue ink, "Thank you, Mr. Johnston, stay strong!" I knew right then and there that this is what I wanted to do.

I have a favorite word: **UNDETERRED.** I love that word. Webster's Dictionary defines undeterred as **"persevering with something despite setbacks."** I keep it on a Post-it note on the wall behind my computer in my office. I have had that note on my wall for years. It's fallen off a few times and gathered dust; I have had to rewrite it, yet it's still there to remind me. It stares at me each day like an old friend hoping to keep me from becoming distracted from my purpose and those who need me most. Far too often, we are so burdened by what daily life has thrown at us we rush past those who mean the most. In a sense, all we really have is this moment. When we dwell on the past or look too far into the future, we miss what is right in front of us - life.

"The future is uncertain, but the end is always near."
-Jim Morrison

In the early hours of October 4, 2016, I would come to fully understand in sharp, painful detail what the word, "*undeterred*" meant and, more importantly, how significant the weight and magnitude this word would carry for me. That empty, desolate day in 2016 forever altered the trajectory of my life and those I care about the most.

In deciding to write this book, I had to answer the question, "why?" What was my overall objective, and what was I trying to accomplish? I am confident as you work your way through the chapters, you will discover my motivation, my inspiration, and my ultimate goal for this endeavor. Better yet, I hope you will find something in my story that resonates with you and helps you gain new awareness, insight, or perspective in your own life.

Not a day goes by where I don't encounter someone who is hurting or dealing with substance abuse and addiction. Often, it's about someone they love who has the addiction, and they are simply collateral damage, held prisoner to the seduction and cravings so strong that the ones they love become indifferent to the pain they are inflicting. I feel compelled, as difficult as it will be, to make sure the experiences and events I have witnessed don't go to waste. There is much to be learned from someone else's unfortunate circumstances, and with that, I have a very important and timely story to tell.

In 2017, approximately 7% of the U.S. population experienced a significant depression episode, according to the National Institute of

Mental Health (NIMH). Depression is the world's leading cause of disability. In the United States, suicide rates have jumped 33 percent from 1999-2017, according to the National Vital Statistics System, and nearly one in five Americans live with a mental health issue according to the NIMH. On top of this, 20% of Americans who have depression and/or anxiety issues also have a substance abuse disorder. In 2018, according to the non-profit Trust for America's Health, more than 150,000 people died in the U.S collectively from drug overdoses, alcohol, and suicide. **Alarmingly this is a 51% increase over the past decade.**

Depression and mental health can all trigger or be a gateway into substance abuse and vice versa. Unfortunately, an existing market is in place for a story such as ours to be told. Many Americans are understandably hurting and in pain but numbing the weight of life's stress is clearly not the answer.

In the early chapters of this book, I will cover, in detail, that fateful day in 2016, how addictions and substance abuse slowly crept into the fabric of our family, and how the hideous specter of death presented itself. Later in the book, I will share how the game of golf, for a while, distracted me from the pain and suffering addiction and death had created. Chaos and tragedy can spawn beautiful ideas from impassioned people. I promise you will see that good can come from bad, and how I am still learning about my purpose and meaning in life. I will also provide some suggestions to help those struggling with trauma, substance abuse and addiction.

I wish to strongly emphasize the fact that this book is a recollection of memories, moments, and feelings from my point of view only. Everyone deals with hardship, grief, and loss in their own way, so I am leaving out many important people in my life as I do not feel comfortable making any assumptions about how they feel or felt. While I will describe specific events and moments in detail, I will also attempt to respect and honor their privacy. I will commit to being as accurate as I can. Memories do fade; however, please trust my intentions are nothing but good. I hope this story will help those who need it in their healing process and provide some comfort as we all evolve and grow from this together.

I am not a psychologist, a neuroscientist, a theologian, or a doctor. I am a dad, son, coach, entrepreneur, brother, voter, friend, and neighbor. I am very much like many of you, I would assume. I grew up in Iowa City, Iowa, and went to high school in Solon, Iowa, a small yet thriving community just a few miles north of Iowa City. I graduated from Marshalltown Community College (MCC) in Marshalltown, Iowa in 1986 and the University of Northern Iowa in 1989 with a finance degree. Basketball and golf were my sports, and I was fortunate enough to play both at MCC. I call Cedar Rapids home now and enjoy the Midwest life even though I really enjoy seeing the world.

I can't promise to have all the answers, but I will make one promise to you throughout this book, I will be honest and truthful. I will open old, raw wounds exposing myself to temporary pain, but I am sincere in my belief that this story will give you hope that there are other ways to deal with adversity. **I believe that you are always free to tell yourself a new story about your past.** You can control the narrative of your life, no matter how unpleasant or painful looking back becomes.

Life's experiences can be a very efficient teacher. You never take an exam to obtain designations behind your name. Yet, it's pass or fail every single minute of each day for the rest of your life. The results of your final exam will be revealed long after your death in the legacy you leave. Inheritances are spent, but legacies last forever. What will your legacy be?

We all know how fragile life can be and how fortunate we are to be alive; I am just not sure we all truly appreciate what we have until it's gone. Unfortunate events, when they happen to others, allow us to pause for a brief moment and reflect on our own lives, relieved it wasn't us. We soon distract ourselves by moving on to our daily grind, possibly forgetting or burying the unfortunate event that occurred. That is until it happens to you.

October 4, 2016

It was a Tuesday, a day that started out like any other.
Another crisp, gorgeous fall day in the heartland of
America. A great day to play golf. The nerves were in full
force that morning at the Johnston house. Our youngest
son, Roman, had left for school on the morning bus. I was
getting ready to take our middle son, Ian, to meet his golf
team before circling back home to pick up my wife,
Prudence, who was preparing the items we would need for
what I imagined would be a long, stressful day on the golf
course. Ian's team was heading out to compete for their
High School District Golf Tournament at Pheasant Ridge
Golf Course in Cedar Falls, Iowa. A fair test of golf laid out
on over 6,600 yards of Iowa terrain.

Ian was a sophomore at Prairie High School and was playing
the number one position that day. He was out to exorcise
some golf demons as the previous year, when he was a
freshman, he tripled his last hole at Districts and missed
qualifying for State by two shots. The hour-long drive to
the golf course was going to be a great opportunity to talk
with my wife about our plans for later that day and what we
were going to do if the team qualified for the Iowa State
High School Golf Championships the following week.
Prairie has had many State Championship appearances in

wrestling, football, basketball, track, and volleyball. Yet one sport had alluded them since the records had been kept. Boys Golf had never qualified for State, and this year felt like it was the year. We had a great group of seniors and juniors that gelled together well as the season unfolded.

Most parents can relate to the tremendous ups and downs associated with sports. It's a classic love/hate relationship. Like many parents of athletes, I envisioned that day being no different. I would soon find out that the stress of lipped out putts and bad drives would be replaced by something much more ominous. There was an odd stillness in the air that morning that I have reflected on only as time has passed.

I pulled into the school parking lot, where the team meets for away tournaments. It's appropriately called the "bus barn" as it's where the school keeps the buses when not in use. It was around 6:30 am. As we pulled in, I saw the usual sights: other parents and students, as well as the Boys Golf coach, Erik Columbus. Coach Columbus has been the golf coach at Prairie High School since 2003, working first with the girl's program. He had heard about Ian a few years earlier and had always been anxiously awaiting the chance to coach him. As a parent, I couldn't think of a better person for my son to play for.

I hit the button to release the trunk and hopped out of the truck. As I climbed out, I raised my hand to wave at Coach Columbus. He returned the wave. I could see he was busy trying to get everything together, organizing coolers full of food and golf clubs that were in disarray. The excitement of the upcoming day weighed heavily on the faces of everyone. As I look back at the moments and hours that happened next, my memories are fragmented. Some moments are seared into my brain, never to be forgotten. Yet, at the same time, there are moments that I don't recall at all. Shock will do that to you.

As I was taking Ian's clubs from the trunk, my phone rang. I looked down at my phone to check the caller ID and realized it was a call from our oldest son Seth's dad, Paul. Seth was from Prudence's first marriage. Receiving a call from Paul this early in the morning on a weekday was not a regular occurrence, so part of me knew it probably wasn't going to be good news. I put Ian's clubs down and answered the phone. My instinct was correct. It was that dreaded call you get – the call that all parents fear - where you know from that point on, **nothing will ever be the same.**

In the state of Iowa, there were 180 Opioid-related deaths in 2016. In the early morning of October 4, 2016, at the age of 23, our son Seth, became a part of that statistic.

Not a statistic to us but a statistic nonetheless; he was dead.

I opened my mouth to tell Ian, and then it dawned on me. This wouldn't be fair to him or the team. Not after everything they have worked for. I decided, in the moment, nothing positive would be gained from letting him know his brother had died. Obviously, I hadn't been prepared for this; there isn't a handbook on what to do in these situations. I was making it up on the fly: no judgment, no second-guessing, no right or wrong. I just knew that this wasn't the time or the place.

I wanted Ian to enjoy his day without burden or impediment. Still in shock, I turned away from Ian, got in the truck, and drove off. I never told Ian that I loved him or wished him and the team luck like I always did. I just turned and got in the truck and drove home. Like a zombie. How was I going to tell my wife that our son was dead? How is this possibly happening? This had to be a horrible dream.

The next memory I have is walking into the house and seeing my wife ready to go and dressed in a black and orange Prairie golf shirt with her golf hat pulled down over her head. She looked like all the other golf moms preparing to walk 18 holes on a beautiful day talking to other parents about golf and life. I couldn't speak; I was trembling profusely. I was at a complete loss of words. She instantly knew something terrible had happened. I struggled to get three words out of my mouth, "Seth is dead."

It was the single worst moment of my life. Ten minutes ago, I was living the American Dream. At fifty years old, I had a family, a nice house, and a successful business - I was on top of the world. It sounds selfish, I know, but I was.

One thing I have learned is that there is no template or guide to describe the intense sorrow and helplessness that you go through when something like this happens. You just react to whatever emotions overtake you at the moment and are helpless to understand or reason clearly. Survival instincts kick in, and you seem to have a heightened sense of awareness.

We both fell to the ground clutching each other for support and trying to let the gravity of the situation resonate within us. We picked ourselves up after what felt like a brief moment, yet seemingly we had both aged years, maybe decades at that time. So many powerful images flash through your mind, and heavy emotions tear at your heart during those moments.

Seth had been found, by his dad, in a motel room in Waterloo, Iowa. He had been staying there while working for his dad in the construction business. My wife and I collected ourselves, got in the car, and headed out to the motel where it all happened.

As I stood in the parking lot of the motel where Seth was found, I realized something profound. Ian was trying to qualify for State approximately two miles from where his older brother was found dead of a heroin overdose. Within two miles of each other. Later on, you will see the significance and how this all came together for us. For now, I was thinking about trying to stabilize the situation and wondering how the hell I was going to tell Ian and Roman their big brother was gone forever.

At that moment, golf seemed so distant and unimportant to me. I never thought about Ian and how his day was going, or what he felt when he walked up to the first tee, driver in hand, his biggest fans nowhere to be seen. His fifteen-year-old brain processing, wondering if something bad had happened because mom and dad never missed a meet. Roman, I am sure was enjoying another day of seventh grade, excited to jump off the bus at the end of the day and see one of us at the bottom of the hill to pick him up. Both of them were completely unaware of how much life was about to change. We all are in the moments before these events happen.

At the motel, we were met by Seth's dad, Paul, and the Sheriff, along with medical personnel. The ambulance with Seth's body had left a few moments prior. Many questions were asked, and all of us were still in a state of shock. At one point, the police asked if we wanted to go into Seth's room. I was the only one who went back into the room. Paul had been the one to find Seth, and he didn't feel the need to go back. I respected and understood that. All I could think of was how he must have felt finding Seth. My heart went out to him and still does.

Walking into Seth's motel room was surreal. It is one of those moments I mentioned before that will live with me for the rest of my life. A small circular table sat to the right of the sliding glass door. An empty beer can and a cigarette ashtray sat on the table next to some paperwork and a receipt from a laundromat. The Sheriff said there was no reason to suspect foul play, the door to the room was locked from the inside, as was the sliding glass door pointing towards the parking lot.

A TV and some boxes containing his personal belongings laid in the corner of the room to my left. A chair was positioned a few feet from the table, turned towards the small bed to my right. I later learned that was the chair Seth was found in, slumped over, hands in his lap, resting peacefully. As I looked over to his neatly made bed, it dawned on me that he never made it that far. The poison in his veins robbed him of even the slight pleasure of making it to his bed.

What I saw next hit me hard, brutally hard. As I write these words, I know it is the first time I am sharing them with anyone. I planned to take this memory to my grave. I didn't want to be vulnerable again to the feelings I had at that moment. In the years since Seth's death, it has become clear that the only way to stop being vulnerable is to stop caring, and that is something I cannot do. I care about Seth, and I love him more than ever. So, I am going to tell you what I saw.

"Vulnerability sounds like truth and feels like courage. Truth and courage aren't always compatible, but they are never weaknesses."
- Brene Brown

On his bed was his belt. The belt was crudely formed into a tourniquet. Lifeless, positioned as if it was gently tossed on the bed after being tightly wrapped around his arm. The belt, which I had seen him wear so many times, pulling up his pants, was now the mechanism that assisted in pulling him down to his death. Along with the belt was the skull bandana he wore so often. I put the belt in a box, and I picked up the bandana. I don't know where the belt is today, as we have since moved. The image of it is all I will ever need. As for the bandana, it has been on Ian's golf bag for every tournament since.

The sight of the belt is significant to me. A belt can be used to assist you in life and, at the same time, can be used to kill you. Like a rope that can be used to pull you up yet that same rope can be used to hang you. It has a dual purpose. As I later pondered larger issues with living and dying, the duality of something as simple as a belt left me in awe. **"That which does not kill us makes us stronger"** is a term we all have heard. Controversial German Philosopher Friedrich Nietzsche has been credited for saying this. I guess the belt represents something like this to me. I wasn't going to let this kill me; it had to make me stronger. The concept of the belt, as you will see later, resurfaces in my story from a whole different perspective yet with potentially the same sinister result.

Seth, unfortunately, died in a very stereotypical way that we are used to seeing presented in movies and the media. A seedy motel in a tough part of town. That's how it ended for him, but that wasn't who he was.

Seth Carnicle

From the moment I met them, Prudence and Seth were a package deal. Seth was always so protective of his mother. I recall once when I was on a date with her, and little Seth was in the back seat in his booster seat. I could feel the laser-like stare on the back of my head. I knew he was keenly aware that I had an interest in his mom, and to get to her, I had to go through him. I always thought it was very cute and innocent that he felt that way as a very quiet little kid. What a delightful little boy he was!

Seth as a Toddler

The three of us constructed a life together, and a few years later came Ian, then Roman, a dog, a cat, and a new house. Like all brothers, they had their ups and downs. But Ian and Roman had a special bond with Seth. Seth was always trying to stay active in his younger brothers' lives. He would attend Roman's wrestling tournaments and follow Ian's golf successes. Seth was so damn proud of those two. He would often brag about them to his friends and acquaintances.

Prudence & I with Seth, Ian, and Roman

I grew up as a huge Iowa Hawkeye fan. My father, David, was the team physician for the Iowa Men's Basketball team for many years. Doc, as he was nicknamed, worked at the University of Iowa in the Student Health Department. Hall

18

of Fame basketball coach, Lute Olson (who recently passed away at the age of 85 on 8/27/2020), asked my dad in the mid-seventies to help with home games first. It then evolved to sitting at the end of the bench and ultimately traveling with the team. My dad worked under Lute, George Raveling, Dr. Tom Davis, and ultimately Steve Alford. He was elected to the University of Iowa Athletics Hall of Fame class of 2003, the same Hall of Fame class as iconic wrestling coach Dan Gable. My dad has the unique honor of being in two collegiate athletic Hall of Fame Classes. The University of Iowa as the basketball team physician and at Coe College in Cedar Rapids, Iowa as a two-sport athlete. Growing up with the great Ronnie Lester, Kevin Boyle, Brad Lohaus, and others shooting baskets in our driveway was awesome as a youth. To say that Hawkeye Basketball was a huge part of my childhood would be an understatement, and I wanted to pass on my love for the Hawks to my children.

Seth loved his Iowa Hawkeyes, and we attended many games as he was growing up. Seth would go with us to the Big Ten Tournaments, the NCAA Tournaments, and countless home games at Carver Hawkeye Arena in Iowa City. Many times, he was sitting with grandpa by the tunnel, giving high fives to players as they ran out to the court. Many of them knew who he was at that age. Seth actually got to go into the locker room after a few games, thanks to grandpa. He must have felt like a rock star.

Young Seth at an Iowa Hawkeye Basketball Game

When Seth was seven, my wife and I took him on a trip. This trip will always be special to me. The three of us flew to New York to catch the Hawks playing in the NCAA Tournament in Long Island. The year was 2000-01. Iowa had a decent regular season led by Indiana transfer Luke Recker and Reggie Evans, who would lead the Big Ten in rebounding that year. Iowa ended the season losing six of their last seven Big Ten games. Nonetheless, the Hawks battled back to win the Big Ten Conference Championships with four straight wins over Northwestern, Ohio State, Penn State, and Indiana. We had watched every second of all four games.

Iowa received the automatic bid to the NCAA Tournament that year. We were hesitant to go because my wife was seven months pregnant with Ian. Nonetheless, we went unaware that the trip was going to be very eventful. Iowa defeated Creighton in round one as a number seven seed and was scheduled to play Kentucky, one of the blue bloods. At the time, Kentucky was coached by Tubby Smith. Seth was so excited to see them play, especially future NBA star Tayshaun Prince. The game was at The Nassau Coliseum in Uniondale, New York. We lost a good game, 92-79.

After the game, my wife mentioned she was not feeling very well, and I went to my dad to get some guidance. After a short time at a local hospital, it was determined that everything was ok with her and the baby. The problem or concern was that we were not scheduled to fly out until late the next day, and my dad was worried about leaving us behind in New York as he headed back with the team on a flight to Iowa later that evening. So, my dad and John Strief - the team trainer and a great family friend - pulled a few strings and were able to get us three on the team charter flight back.

Wow not only were we extremely grateful, but we were very excited to go back with the team. I can still see Seth sitting with Luke Recker and Reggie Evans, eating ice cream, and talking Iowa hoops. I am forever grateful to those two legendary Hawkeye heroes for taking the time to show Seth some attention. It would have been easy for them to sulk and be down after a loss, but they were great, and so was the whole team for that matter.

Seth (Age 7) with Future NBA Player Reggie Evans at Carver-Hawkeye Area

Seth was a tremendous basketball player. Better than he gave himself credit for. I had the honor to coach all the boys, but Seth had the most athleticism of any of them. He finished 10th individually in the two-mile race in 8th grade at the Middle School State Cross Country meet in 2008. The 8th grade team was crowned State Champions that year. Seth could have been excellent in any sport, but there was something about basketball he really enjoyed.

Basketball was his love. He would spend hours in the driveway working on his crossover and Euro step, which was gaining popularity in the NBA. Kobe Bryant, Lebron James, and Allen Iverson were his heroes along with the old school legends he heard me discuss frequently, Larry Bird and Michael Jordan, to name a few. He would collect basketball cards and had at least two dozen jerseys from his favorite NBA players and teams.

Seth in his Carmelo Anthony Jersey

A game his freshman year still brings back tremendous feelings when I reflect on it now. Prairie High School was playing conference rival Iowa City High at the Prairie

23

Gymnasium. The game was close all the way and was tied late in the 4th quarter. After two free throws from them, we had the ball with six seconds left. I was nervous watching Prairie inbound the ball and dribble to half court. Seth set up in the far corner to get the ball and caught it with two seconds left. Like he had practiced thousands of times in our driveway, he caught the ball, pivoted to the basket, and let it fly. The ball split the net as the horn sounded. Seth had won the game on a last-second three-pointer! We were all screaming and hugging each other as his teammates mobbed him in congratulations.

I recently came across the DVD of that game while we were moving last August. I plan on watching it for the first time since his death after I complete this book. Photographs have been challenging enough to look at, but videos of him I am still trying to muster the courage to watch. I have boxes of videos I haven't watched yet. Heroin may have taken Seth, but it cannot and will not take my memories of him, that I am sure.

We had many heated games of 1 on 1 when I still could beat him. He used to get so mad when he lost. The younger Seth used this anger and frustration to get better. As he got older, his anger and frustrations morphed into substance abuse. Sadly, his addiction to alcohol and drugs grew stronger than his love for basketball.

Seth in His Prairie Hawk Basketball Jersey (4th Grade)

I recall coaching a seventh-grade basketball game when he turned the ball over and looked at me on the court and cried. I felt terrible for him as most of the other kids did not act that way. He always seemed to be pretty hard on himself, and when the ball didn't bounce his way, he often overreacted and got upset. Not every time, but often enough that I considered it an issue, yet I assumed he'd just

25

outgrow. Maybe I only noticed at the time because I was dad?

Seth was very good academically until around his sophomore year when his experimentation with alcohol and drugs began. His grades in middle school were excellent. I recently came across his report card from the 2007-2008 school year. Seth was in 8th grade:

Language Arts	B-
Math	B
American History	B-
Science	B-
Applied Tech	A
PE	A
Spanish	B

He liked pretty much all of the classes he took, and the majority of his reviews were positive. Most of his issues in the 4th-7th grade were attention and focus issues. In 5th grade, his teacher noted on the report card, "He can get emotional quite easily and gets frustrated." In 6th grade, "Seth has a difficult time staying focused on a task. He is extremely sensitive to teacher suggestions." I don't think, to be honest, he was much different than most kids around this time. I shudder to think what my report cards were like as I had attention and focus issues as well, still do.

It is important to understand that I am by no means trying to be critical or negative of Seth as this story unfolds. I believe we must look back and try to analyze the data we have to identify when issues started with Seth and observe any negative patterns. What do we have to lose?

Freedoms & Fear

I love Seth. I love him enough to tell these difficult stories so others can learn from them. I also believe a more accurate description of him for better or worse was needed to continue his legacy as he, unfortunately, can't add to it anymore. I have many good memories and stories of Seth; it's just a sad reality that my most recent ones stand out for the wrong reasons.

Seth, like all teenagers, was excited to grow up. He wanted to stay out later than before, ask a girl to a school dance, and get a cell phone. He wasn't much different than most of us during those years. Yet when I look back at those moments, more clarity has come into view. Seth always asked for his "freedoms" I like to call it. He always stressed to us that all the other kids were getting "freedoms" and that he wanted them as well.

Teenage Seth

In hindsight, I realize Seth seemed to trail his peer group emotionally by a year or two. It seemed like he was a little less mature and a little less emotionally ready to handle those freedoms we granted to him. My wife and I discussed this on more than one occasion as he was growing up. Each child matures at a different pace and handles responsibilities differently. This makes parenting very challenging. How soon do we give "freedoms," and how much of them do we give?

The other personality trait I saw from him was he was more likely to be a follower than a leader. I think he had a hard time saying "no" to people. He gave in to peer pressure too easily. The freedoms granted to him turned out to be an invitation to experiment with alcohol soon followed by marijuana.

Seth had absolutely no fear. No fear of authority, teachers, parents, jail, and eventually, death. Often that ability to have no fear is an asset going through life. But at some point, most of us develop a social "off" button. We don't steal because we don't want to get caught and get in trouble. We don't drive drunk because we don't want our name in the paper or to lose our license or, worse yet, to kill someone. We don't do drugs because they are illegal and can be very bad for you, and you may spend time behind bars. We have a social filter, the ability to grasp right from wrong, to have a guilty conscience. As I later discovered, feeling guilty and having remorse are not the same thing.

The young Seth had a certain fight in him, a competitive drive; however, the older, addicted Seth lost the ability and desire to notice everything caving in around him. The helplessness of watching a loved one spiral out of control is torturous. Especially when it's mostly self-created, it's literally a slow-motion train wreck. This train wreck for us lasted eight long years.

Around 16-17 years old, he became more paranoid and delved into all types of conspiracy theories like the Illuminati, chemtrails, and other internet-driven hysteria. It became more than just a youthful, curious mind exploring life's biggest questions. He really believed these things, and they started to affect him adversely. The Seth we knew was replaced by someone else. I simply did not recognize him anymore. Although he was never diagnosed with a mental illness, I am now convinced he was a good candidate. Seth did see a psychiatrist a few times during high school. I don't recall exactly when, but I do remember it did little to help him. He wasn't willing to accept help, as I am not sure he perceived a problem.

It got so bad around this time; we had to hide the valuables and lock doors at night. It wasn't that I was so afraid he would harm us as it was the fear that people he associated with would break into our house to steal money for drugs. The kid's video games, Xbox, other stuff started to disappear. Seth's addictions were slowly creeping into the foundation of our family that we had worked so hard to build. I was unsure where to turn for help and tried without avail waiting for him to fix this himself.

There was a morning when I was preparing to go to work, and I realized Seth, who should have been on his way to school, was still sleeping downstairs. I ran into his room and yelled at him to get up. He awoke like he saw a ghost. He was utterly terrified and had no clue where he was. I said, "Seth, you are late for school. Let's go I will drive you." I waited a few moments for him to collect his stuff, and we dashed out the door. As we jumped into the car, he said he was very thirsty, and I noticed his mouth was so dry that he could barely speak. I had a sense something was wrong. As we drove away, he very quietly turned to me and said, "Dad, why are there elephants on the horizon?" I thought he was kidding. He wasn't. I soon realized that when he asked me another question that made no sense.

I called my wife and told her we were driving straight to urgent care in Cedar Rapids to see what was in his system. It turned out he had OD'd on Benadryl. Huh? I had never heard of this happening. Looking back, I now believe he was simply using the internet to find household items to feed his addictions. In this case, I think Benadryl was being used to help him sleep or come down after getting high. I don't really know, to be honest. This was when we had to start hiding cough syrup and all other medications.

Seth's sophomore year in high school was beset with many red flags that now I can see were early warning signs. I have too many stories to tell and wish not to get bogged down in negativity, but I am highlighting a few to give some clarity to our dilemma. Alcohol was more than likely where the substance abuse got its spark. Marijuana was fuel to the flame, followed by cocaine, which was like pouring gasoline on an already raging inferno. Seth ended up dying in a motel room from heroin, but heroin wasn't where it started. The unnerving part of all this is these are only the times we caught him or know about which I assume represented a tiny percentage of his actual experimentation with drugs and alcohol.

Seth's Freshman Year School Photo

34

I recall a time my wife and I were at an industry conference out of town, Ian and Roman were staying with family friends. It was Seth's sophomore year. After we got back, I knew something had happened at our house. After some tense discourse back and forth and a few threats, he admitted he had a party at our house. That in itself, I probably could have lived with. After all, I was a teenager once too.

I am sure there were times when my parents had their suspicions about parties thrown at their house, and they would have been correct. I have three brothers, my older brothers Steve and Scott, and my younger brother Dan. I am not going to sit here and say that my parents' house was never used occasionally to host a teenage party. In the mid-'80s, growing up in small-town Iowa, that was just what kids did. The difference is that no one ever died. Not one of my high school friends OD'd on drugs or alcohol. I am not condoning what we did; I am just saying, for the most part, we drank beer and stayed out of trouble. Never were drugs involved, ever. Unfortunately, at parties today, the drugs are plentiful, and they are loaded with crap that can fuel a jet engine.

Seth admitted to us that at the party in our basement, he tried cocaine. Wow, this was the first time I had heard this word from Seth. Did I assume alcohol and maybe pot? Sure, but cocaine? I have never even seen cocaine, and here our teenage son was trying it. My wife and I were in shock, to say the least. He claimed it was only once, as they all do. I said, "Seth, the path you are on will lead to one of two places, jail or death" Little did I know I would be right on both counts.

There were times he stuffed the vents in his bathroom with towels to hide the smell of marijuana. The empty beer cans we found hidden under everything and tossed in the backyard. His car often had empty bottles in the back seat and trunk. It seemed the more we looked, the more we found. I knew this was becoming an issue, and it seemed to be only getting worse.

Even with everything going on, we did have a few good moments during this time. Seth graduated High School in 2012. I was so proud of him. We told him that his diploma was something they could never take from him. For a fleeting moment, it looked like we had a positive to enjoy. It was short-lived. Seth was eventually kicked out of our house. I reached a point where it came down to providing a safe environment for our other two boys. Ian was ten, and Roman was eight at the time. It wasn't an easy decision, but it was what we thought was best. We could not allow the toxicity of his lifestyle to affect the rest of the occupants of the house negatively.

Seth's Senior Photo

That summer, we were on vacation in Minnesota, Seth broke into our house. I had told my neighbor about what Seth was dealing with and told him to call me if he saw anything strange as I didn't want him in our house. My neighbor called a few days into our trip and said Seth's car was out front. I called Seth and was surprised he answered the phone. He told me he didn't have a place to stay and decided to stay at our house. He had climbed up our back deck and kicked in the back porch door. I was extremely upset and told him to get out. He said he wasn't going to leave.

I had a friend who did security on the weekends, and he had an intimidating looking badge. He offered to go out and tell him he had to leave. It worked. That day really heightened my concerns and fears for my family. I want to add that Seth had never shown any violence toward any of us, and we really never had any issues with that. He had a short fuse and got frustrated, but I never felt he would harm us in any way, and he never threatened us.

Choices

After high school, Seth bounced around considering his options. The military would have been a great choice; however, Seth was getting more and more into anti-government conspiracies and did not want to defend something he did not trust. He became interested in writing rap lyrics that discussed some of the anti-police rhetoric so often used in the more extreme songs. I saw a tremendous change in him. He was gravitating towards negative, angry influences. More or less blaming everyone around him and never taking accountability or responsibility for his actions.

Seth had a few brushes with the law starting right after High School. Reckless driving in 2012, fifth-degree theft, and public intoxication in 2013. He spent 30 days in jail after being charged with two counts of assault in 2015, and another 48 hours behind bars after an OWI in 2016. In another incident, he, along with two others, broke into a home that belonged to his friend's parents. Yes, the parents of one of the two he was with believe it or not. He claimed he was only driving. However, in the eyes of the law, it doesn't matter. His crime caught up with him after a receipt for a stolen TV was found, signed by Seth, at a pawn shop in Des Moines, Iowa. Being drugged up makes you do some pretty stupid things.

He was arrested, and after a plea bargain, received a short stay in the Linn County Jail. I visited every few days to see how he was doing and made the occasional cash deposits into his account so he could buy stuff if needed. Going to the hearing with our attorney and seeing him escorted in the courtroom wearing an orange jumpsuit with Linn County Jail embossed on the back was tough to handle. Handcuffed, hands in front, embarrassingly looking down. When our eyes met, I had a flood of emotion race over me, and for that moment, both of our eyes simultaneously swelled up with tears. He looked so lost and alone, yet I could still see that delightful little boy deep behind those empty eyes.

It was only a few years ago that I was watching him graduate from Prairie High School with the same color orange in ribbons draped over his shoulders. Wow had things gone south fast. I just wanted to reach out and save him. As I have learned on this addiction journey, only those who WANT to be helped can be helped; everything else is wishful thinking. I was trying to remain optimistic. This was taking a huge toll on all of us.

Seth's High School Graduation (May 2012)

I did take Roman to jail one time to visit Seth. Ian didn't want to go, and I respected how they both felt. I never pressured either one of them. Roman wanted to see what jail was like, and I was hoping I could use the opportunity to make this a deterrent for him and also show Seth we were not giving up on him even with all his issues. His little brother sure brightened his day, and I know the visit was impactful for Roman as well. When my wife and Roman went to pick Seth up after he was released, Roman ran and

jumped into his arms, and they held hands as they walked
back to the car.

Seth and Roman on the Beach in Hilton Head, SC

I wish I had more pictures of Roman and Seth to include as
I write this. However, as I look through my photo albums
and cell phone, I have become painfully aware of the gaps
in time where Seth was not part of our lives. His descent
into substance abuse was so severe that periods of time
would go by where we simply wouldn't hear from him at all.

Eventually, Seth ended up in prison in 2015 for an assault
that I won't spend time revisiting. I was in northern
Minnesota on our annual FLA (Fisherman Liar's
Association) trip with a group of men that have been going
for over 40 years. Seth called me in a frantic voice,
explaining he had done something bad and was very scared

of what was about to happen. I could tell in his voice for the first time he was genuinely terrified of the magnitude of his poor choices. After he explained to me the context of his situation, I called my lawyer and told him not to say anything. Long story short, the result was a plea bargain and prison time. While incarcerated, Seth would often write to his little brothers. Here is one such touching and heartfelt letter Seth wrote just two months before his death:

August 2016

Dear Roman,

How have you been
doing buddy? As you know
I am In prison but I
shouldnt be gone too long.
I should be done with
everything In 20 months.
Im sorry I cant be there
for you and Ian but I have
to get this out of the way.
I can tell you about
everything when I get out.
I know I havent been
the best big brother all
the time, but when Im
with you guys I have fun,
you and Ian give me
something to look forward
to when I get out. Anyways
write me back, I love
you guys.

Love
Seth
Seth Carver

44

We had purchased a condo in Clearwater, Florida, a few years back, we had been traveling there quite a bit for Ian's golf career, and it was a nice getaway for us. In July 2016, we were shopping at the mall in Clearwater on a beautiful, sun-filled afternoon, and as we were leaving, my phone rang. It was my lawyer, Tom Viner, and he was excited to share some news with me regarding Seth. He told us that Seth was going to be released early and thought he would let us know. I could tell in his voice, although happy for us, he was thinking the same thing I was. Seth was better off in prison. It gave him daily structure, responsibilities, and a place to lay his head. I turned to my wife and said, "This isn't good news at all. I don't have a good feeling about this."

Seth was soon gone after his release from prison. Not only was he released from the bars of society's imprisonment, but he was also released from the internal prison he had created for himself. He was, finally, truly free. For many of us, this earthly, material existence is a daily struggle full of pain and suffering. For Seth, it seemed every step forward was followed by two steps backward.

I would like to say my last words to him were, "I love you," but they weren't. My last words to him, as we were standing in our garage a few weeks prior to his death, were, "You need to quit drinking." Not very inspiring or eloquent, but

45

at that moment, upset and angry, that is what I said. In a way, I was saying, "I love you."

Two Roads

The hour-long car ride back from the motel seemed like only a few minutes. My wife and I spent the majority of the time in the car answering the phone and making calls. The immediate outpouring of support was unreal, yet the pain and anguish for those Seth left behind was to be a formidable opponent in the days, months, and years to come.

As we approached our neighborhood, we stopped to pick up Roman as he got off the bus. He jumped into the back of the car, and we drove the very short distance up the hill to our house. We had agreed not to tell him about Seth until Ian got home. Doing this as a family was the goal. I had to drive to the high school to pick Ian up as he was finished with his golf meet. I can honestly say I don't recall much from the time I left the house to when Ian and I walked back into the house. What I do remember was that Ian looked pretty dejected and upset as we drove home. I am sure the tension and stillness in the car must have given him some concern, yet I have to believe he was pretty wrapped up in the day's events on the golf course.

As we pulled into the driveway and went into the garage, I took a moment to pause and look at the basketball hoop we put in for Seth. A tattered Iowa Hawkeye foam cushion around the base of the pole. The net torn and hanging loosely, beat up by the many shots over the years. I thought of the time Uncle Mike had fallen off the roof trying to install a light so Seth could shoot all night. So many evenings, we could hear Seth pounding the pavement working on all his moves. I could briefly see him now looking back at me.

Ian proceeded to tell us that he felt terrible because he doubled bogeyed his last hole, and the team missed qualifying for State by a few shots. That was two years in a row that Ian lost his chances for State on the very last hole, and he was devastated. On any other day, I would agree this was devastating, but on this day I had far worse news. We hugged Ian, kissed him, and told him we loved him.

The next moment was the one I had been dreading all day. I called my dad earlier as we drove to the motel where Seth was found and asked for his advice on how to break the news to Ian and Roman. As a doctor, he has had plenty of experience with living and dying. I trusted he could give me some help in how and what to say to them. He gave me some great advice, "Jeff, sit them down and tell them the truth of what happened. Most importantly, and I emphasize MOST IMPORTANTLY after you tell them you need to shut the hell up!" My dad, fully aware that I like to talk, was adamant that I allow the boys time to digest this horrible news and also time to ask questions.

As my dad instructed, I told the boys to sit down on the couch as I had some bad news for them. I looked at them both, cleared my voice, slightly trembling, and said, "Boys - Seth died this morning. I wish I could tell you something different." I didn't say another word. It was very calm and quiet for what seemed like an eternity as both boys looked up at us for more information. Tears swelled up in their eyes. I had nothing more to add, and I didn't want to talk. Finally, Ian asked, almost ashamedly, "How did he die, drugs?" I paused and said, "Yeah, drugs."

I am sure Roman's young mind couldn't really process the implications and what death really meant. They were both there through Seth's addictions and experienced all the stress and anguish that rips through a family. His death was, in a way, very predictable yet frustratingly preventable at the same time.

The next words out of my mouth came unrehearsed and spontaneously. Brutally honest yet poignant. I said, "Boys, there are only two roads we can go down now. One road of anger, despair, and hatred, and we will become addicts ourselves, or we can go down a road of inspiration and hope, making sure this day will change our lives and those around us for the positive and for the better. I am choosing the second road, and I ask you to join me".

I am sincere in that it rolled off my tongue that smoothly and with tremendous honesty. No response or commitment was needed from them. I was their mentor, their leader. I had to come up with something that showed them we can survive this, and we must. *Undeterred.*

All of us, at some point, will be offered the opportunity to go down one of the two roads. The proverbial fork in the road. It could be related to work, relationships, personal commitments, or something else. I often told all three boys that you are either improving or getting worse each day. It's impossible to stay the same. It can't happen. You either grow, learn, and challenge yourself, or you simply allow yourself to erode like a dying plant. Reacting negatively to what life throws at you is no way to live. I have been fortunate to have a very positive attitude and outlook my whole life. Seth's death didn't change that at all. If anything, for me, it reinforced the fact that I MUST be positive in each moment and always find ways to evolve.

The Process of Death

Roman was thirteen, and Ian was fifteen at the time of Seth's passing. The concept of death from a child's perspective is very different from an adult's understanding. I needed to be cognizant of this as I navigated my own emotional stages of death.

According to the Institute of Medicine (US) Committee for the Study of Health Consequences of the Stress of Bereavement, from the ages of 12 through adolescence, a few common characteristics can be found in dealing with death:

- Death is now viewed abstractly and subjectively.
- There is a strong egocentrism and a tendency to think of themselves as immortal.
- Subjective curiously develops: "What is the meaning of life?", "What is my special mission?" "Why doesn't anyone besides me understand the implications of life and death?"
- Death is often romanticized as beautiful and tragic, paradoxically a gesture or statement that will somehow endure.
- Due to television and movies, they see loss experienced through death as easy to deal with.

- Although there is much objective philosophizing about death, it is still seen as something that happens to others.

In a paper by Jan-Louise Godfrey in July 2017 titled, "The Impact of Sibling Death on Adolescent Psychosocial Development and Psychological Wellbeing" she concluded, "Adolescent sibling bereavement is often a traumatic experience that may be compounded by other contextual factors and may lead to the complication of the grief process. The loss of a sibling during adolescence has the capacity to impact the surviving sibling's identity development." **Sibling loss has been identified as one of the most tragic and least understood events that can occur for an adolescent** (Balk 1991; Hogan Desantis,1992). I knew I had to be very careful in how I dealt with this and also others around me, especially children.

Recently, Roman and I were having a good father/son talk about stuff. Conversations many parents have with their children. I sensed, at 16, he was having a few issues he wanted to get off his chest. Roman claims I am hard to talk to because I am too positive. He will often walk up to me and gently put his hand over my mouth and say, "Dad, I love you, but don't talk." I always laugh when he does that.

This time Roman said, "Dad, I just haven't gotten over Seth's death yet, and I need more time." It came out of the blue and floored me as I assumed all was good because he is a straight A student and has never, I mean never, been in trouble.

As a parent, it made me appreciate that there is always more to our kids. We get consumed with living in our "bubble," yet we need to genuinely listen to them. *Attention can redeem almost anything in the present.* I became very interested to hear him out. After I listened without judgment, I told him that It's unfair to him to think he will ever "get over" Seth's death. It's an unrealistic expectation setting him up for inevitable disappointment.

Another more efficient way is to learn to live with his death. Use him as a guide to get you through tough times. He only really truly dies when we stop thinking and talking about him. I believe this to be true. I understand everyone deals with grief in their own way. We all have different coping mechanisms to deal with adversity or tragedy. For me, and I can only speak for myself, I need to chase Seth every day. Have him out front running, and I am trying to catch him yet, knowing I can't. This works for me. I am not sure what I will do if I catch him, similar to the dog chasing the truck. Nonetheless, I am chasing him to this day, unwilling to stop. *Undeterred.*

My point to Roman was that I didn't want to sugarcoat this for him but to try to arm him with the ability to look at things differently. A fresh new perspective. Yes, we miss Seth terribly. However, I will not allow myself the possibility to have my suffering be a disadvantage or excuse in my life. My suffering will be my opportunity (I borrowed this quote from Viktor Frankl.)

I have become a bit of an obsessive reader since Seth died. I average about 2-4 books per month. I have ADD (Attention Deficit Disorder), so it's hard for me to sit down and read just one book all the way through. I often read 3-5 books at one time. I can't explain why I do this or how it makes sense, but for me, that's how I read. For me to read a book in one sitting, it must grab my attention completely.

One book I read start to finish was Man's Search for Meaning by Viktor Frankl. I won't give a book report, but I will say it was a very inspirational book for me. It's a 1946 book chronicling his time as a prisoner in Nazi concentration camps during World War II. His idea of Logotherapy as a type of psychological analysis that emphasizes a "will to meaning" resonated with me. He submits we can find meaning in life in three different ways:

- By creating a work or doing a deed
- By experiencing something or encountering someone
- By the attitude we take towards unavoidable suffering

The last one really made sense to me. It was sort of my point with Roman and his trying to get over Seth's death. Suffering is unavoidable, and in knowing this, our attitude towards suffering when it inevitably happens will determine our happiness in the life we have left. Deep stuff, I know. Death will often push or lead you to explore deep things. I will cover my evolution of self and meaning in the last few chapters in this book.

I learned of Stoicism in college and always felt an attraction to that way of thinking. The Stoic philosophy of personal ethics with logic and reason always seemed interesting to me. It just appeared logical to develop this type of attitude and perspective on life, and I am convinced it helped me in my professional career, especially early on with so many failures. Stoicism is an ancient philosophy founded in Athens in the 3rd century B.C. Interestingly, there seems to be a Stoic resurgence of sorts these days as I have seen more usage of this philosophy lately than ever before. Especially in sports where we see quotes and comments from the most famous Stoics used frequently. Coaches and players have incorporated this type of thinking, as often the challenges faced in sports are the same challenges faced in life.

We all will suffer at some point. The suffering itself isn't uncommon. The Stoics believe the essence of life is how we choose to respond to the things that happen to us. Bill Belichick, Nick Saban, and Pete Carroll are a few of the top coaches that have described the benefits of incorporating the stoic philosophy into their championship programs. Stoics have said, "the most important thing to remember about pain and suffering is that it is inevitable. It can't be avoided, so don't make it worse by fearing it, worrying about whether it will come, wondering how bad it will be, or praying it will go away." A few Stoic philosophers I particularly enjoy;

"What really frightens and dismays us is not external events themselves, but the way in which we think about them. It is not things that disturb us, but our interpretation on their significance."
- Epictetus

"Today, I escaped anxiety. Or no, I discarded it. Because it was within me, in my own perceptions - not outside."
- Marcus Aurelius, Meditations

We are in a never-ending pursuit of happiness, trying to attain some elusive, consistent, yet always elevating level of satisfaction. Happiness is more commonly associated with a pleasurable experience (buying nice clothes, going on a trip) or a positive emotive peak, like joy or getting high for an addict. As I adjust to this new path I am on, I am equally, if not more interested in attempting to attain **peace** in my life rather than the fleeting moments of happiness. Peace, to me, represents a state of mind. I strive to have a deeper connection to relationships and myself rather than relying on a dependent or materialistic connection. Less is more.

Happiness is a challenging aspiration as we unfortunately continuously compare ourselves to others as if that's some sort of baseline in deciding if you're successful (happy) or not. I need to go no further than social media with the false and pretentious lives promoted so heavily by so many. When we arrive at happiness or success, we are often immensely unprepared to actually enjoy anything achieved that we end up blindly chasing another dream or goal. Not much different than a drug addict needing a stronger high or an alcoholic needing "one more drink" or a compulsive gambler needing "one last bet."

Chasing happiness can be an illusion if you haven't dealt with what's holding you back in the first place. I believe there is no recipe for happiness; what we should be seeking are the skills for avoiding negative emotions and habits, in which happiness should result. It's not that we need to make good choices and decisions all the time; instead, it's essential to avoid the bad ones! A wise friend once said about golf and shooting better scores, "It's less about your great shots and more about avoiding the really horrible ones." So true!

Negative emotions and habits become obstacles to truly reaching personal happiness, joy, and peace. Reducing negative emotions and habits should lessen anxiety and stress, ultimately leading you to a more attainable and sustainable level of personal happiness and eventually peace. It isn't that you can completely avoid all negative emotions; you just want to lessen the lifespan of such feelings when they occur.

Although you may not be able to avoid negative emotions, the good news is you can avoid most negative habits. Some negative habits would be smoking, drinking to excess, unhealthy diet, poor sleep, lying to others and yourself, lack of exercise, excessive news coverage on tv, etc. I think it's fair to say that merely being aware of bad habits will not be sufficient to overcome them, unfortunately. There are many good books I would suggest reading; however, I would defer the self-help, motivational books until you feel you have a better grasp on handling negative emotions and reactions. What good are all the positive books, podcasts, and seminars when you are angry, tired, worried, and full of anxiety all the time? Just my 2 cents worth. Patiently build your strong personal foundation from the bottom up.

Addiction

I am asked all the time by concerned parents and even kids after a speaking engagement, "When did it start?" Seth was given his first prescription in third grade for hyperactivity. He was prescribed a non-stimulant, FDA approved drug, I think it was called Strattera. I can honestly say we didn't notice problems starting until he was officially diagnosed with ADD and switched his prescription from Strattera to the stimulant, Adderall. This isn't an indictment of the medical profession, but I have to be honest once he was diagnosed with ADD and given Adderall we started seeing problems. I was always confused in that he was given Adderall for ADD, yet I have ADD, and I have never taken anything. Times have certainly changed.

When I was younger, the prescribed drug of choice was Ritalin. Beginning in the 1960s, Ritalin was used to treat children with ADHD (Attention Deficit Hyperactivity Disorder). In the U.S., Ritalin is classified as a Schedule II controlled substance, which is used to categorize substances that have a "recognized value but present a high potential for abuse." Adderall falls into this same category. According to the CDC, America diagnoses more children with ADHD than anywhere in the world, approximately 11%, with most of these children being medicated.

In 1990, 600,000 children in the United States were on stimulants. By 2011, that number had grown to 3.5 million, contributing to a $13 billion industry! **Interestingly adults are now the majority of the population taking prescription stimulants, and they are the fastest-growing segment of the ADHD market.** Society itself overall has an ADHD problem, and unless addressed, I can't see this improving, especially with addictions to social media, poor eating habits (refined sugars), obesity rates through the roof, etc.

My dad always joked that my ADD was my superhuman strength that others didn't possess. To me, it was an asset, not a weakness. I don't think Seth looked at it this way. There are often preconceived notions about how someone who is diagnosed ADD behaves. I now try to avoid these stereotypes if I can, especially the negative connotations that go along with them. They can poison and prejudice us in ways that have had horrible historical consequences.

In society, there is this need to label people; we group them together based on one small commonality and then make assumptions about who they are based on those labels. These labels - liberal, gay, atheist, religious, illegal immigrant, even the MAGA (Making America Great Again) movement - aren't elevating humans to a very productive, intelligent discussion on our current and future issues. Just spend a few minutes on social media, I rarely do these days for many reasons. It's not surprising our teen suicide rates and mental health issues are so high with the addiction issues of social media usage.

Labels can be used effectively to clarify a position or acknowledge a belief but shouldn't be used to tear people down or negatively judge them. Alcoholics and addicts are labels used, yet we need to be mindful and sensitive in throwing them around as ammunition or in judgment.

In a recent interview on TV, an alcoholic said, quoting the famous song, Hotel California by The Eagles, "You can check out anytime you like, but you can never leave." He said that's what it's like to be an addict. I thought that was an interesting take on the lyrics. Out of curiosity, I researched what that line actually meant in the song, and let's just say, like many things in life, it is open to interpretation.

One of the early issues we had with Seth wasn't the overuse of the drug itself but him selling it at school. I later learned kids are often stealing mom and dad's many prescriptions and then selling them to friends. Crazy stuff, I know. I distinctly recall the first time this came to my attention on a cold, winter night in December 2010 during Seth's sophomore year. I had coached Seth in youth basketball for many years and became good friends with some of the parents. My coaching ceased when he reached high school, but I remained close to these parents. That night I was in my car, and my cell phone rang. It was the father of one of our players who I respected greatly. He told me his son came home from school and was pretty upset. His son told him Seth was selling his Adderall pills at school. I trusted the source of this information as he would have no reason to make this up. Plus, I had my suspicions as well.

I asked Seth about this, and like most times, we confronted him, he had an excuse or brushed it off as an unfounded rumor. Again, another red flag we should have addressed more aggressively? I wasn't sure what to do. You find out addicts are masters of illusion and are brilliant at concocting stories to make sense of their deceptions and lies. Addiction (the negative definition) is the **"continued use of something despite adverse consequences."** By definition, Seth was an addict, something I couldn't deny for much longer.

The harsh reality is if an addicted person is happy with you, you're probably enabling them. If an addicted person is mad at you, you're probably trying to save their life—quite the paradox. I am sure many of you reading this are nodding your heads in agreement. It is a delicate dance to perform, trying to change negative, harmful behavior, and show someone you love and care for them simultaneously.

One of my main regrets in hindsight was not stepping in and learning in more detail about what Seth was being prescribed, specifically Adderall. We, as parents, need to become more engaged in any medications given to our children! Our children trust us to protect them. Our obligation is to them and not for us to be concerned about offending a Doctor by being inquisitive about medications given to our kids. I don't feel much personal guilt with Seth. However, I do anguish over this when I allow myself the time to do so. I cannot go back in time and do this over, but I do have this moment to bring attention to these issues in the hope it can positively change behavior going forwards.

Roman and Ian don't take anything unless I have had a chance to learn about it and get a second opinion, which luckily for me is my Dad. I admit I had never heard of Adderall, and I did zero research on it. Now when I look up Adderall, it says, "Adderall is an addictive prescription stimulant with effects similar to meth." Meth? WTF! (For those older readers, you may need to ask someone what

WTF stands for, although you probably can figure it out!) The ingredients for Meth are common pills for colds, battery acid, gasoline, lithium, drain cleaner, lantern fuel, and antifreeze, among other toxic and lethal items.

So, Adderall is an addictive prescription stimulant with effects similar to meth? I guess now laid out in those terms, I probably should have at least requested a second opinion. Seth's death certificate has an accidental overdose listed with fentanyl as the cause of death. What the hell was fentanyl?? I had never heard of it. Fentanyl is a powerful synthetic opioid similar to morphine but is 50x to 100x times more powerful. What the hell was an opioid?? I could tell you what a 60-degree sand wedge was or a Scotty Cameron putter but Adderall, Fentanyl, Opioids? I was like many parents entering an arena in which I had no familiarity.

Is addiction a disease? Does an addict have a choice not to use? I am not educated enough on the 'brain science" behind this, but I am quite certain they **always had a choice prior to the first time they used**. Once they became an addict, they may or may not have had a choice, but I know before they started, they sure did. Recently, I became curious about the response I would get if I posed this question on social media; Is addiction a disease or a choice? At the time, I imagined an overwhelming preponderance to the disease answer. Surprisingly, my very unscientific social media poll yielded a result I was not prepared for and forced me to dive into this a bit more. The results were 64% disease and 36% choice. I imagined it to be much higher for the disease approach. I understand this was a relatively small sample of respondents, but it still gave me something to ponder and explore a bit deeper.

We know addiction disrupts certain regions of the brain responsible for motivation, memory, and decision-making and is defined as a disease by most medical associations such as the American Medical Association and the American Society of Addiction Medicine. This book is certainly not the place to have a highly qualified, professional discussion on this topic and most certainly only represents my thoughts and opinions on this, nonetheless, let's take a closer look.

Genetics is the study of genes. Genes are functional units of DNA (deoxyribonucleic acid) that make up the human genome (National Institute on Drug Abuse Aug 2019). Genetic risk factors account for about 50% (depending on which report you read) of the likelihood that an individual will develop an addiction. There are other non-genetic risk factors such as friend associations, impulse and control issues, trauma, age of first use, etc. I will discuss nature vs. nurture again later in the book; however, the more I read and learn about these competing forces, I wonder if maybe it should be proposed as nature *and* nurture? It seems fairly clear that addiction and substance abuse is a marriage of both genetics and your environment and not the result of one or the other. The study of epigenetics is further proof that it's more complicated than we had previously thought. To save myself from embarrassment, that's as technical as I plan to get at this point.

Let's look at alcoholism for a moment. Could it be possible that at a young age, you were told you have an addictive gene, a predisposition to drink alcohol? Adding to this, you were keenly aware your parents and grandparents were alcoholics. Based on that information, you believe the outcome is inevitable; you will become an alcoholic. You are likely looking at this as **"it is what it is"** and not **"what could be?"** I spoke in the introduction that you're always free to tell yourself a new story about your past. In other words, can you avoid addiction and substance abuse simply by "tricking" your brain into believing even if you're predisposed, you are not going to allow addictions and substance abuse to enter your life? Look at this another way. Let's say you have a 100% probability of becoming an alcoholic; however, you were raised on an island with no alcohol, what would happen? My guess is that you would find a way to survive and evolve into a person that alcohol has no control over. In this case, you wouldn't have had a choice as your environment dictated the outcome. Environment is such a key, and I believe for many addicts, a need to "find an island" and strengthen their belief in themselves will go a long way in conquering the daily torture of wondering if this is the day I fall?

I was speaking with a very good friend and alcoholic a while back, and the discussion centered on how this individual had relapsed seven times over the past few years. He kept "falling off the wagon" as they say for many different, seemingly to him, legitimate reasons. I asked him what his plan was going forwards, and he alluded to continuing going to meetings and all the other methods that didn't seem to work. The definition of insanity is doing the same thing over and over and expecting different results.

I asked him, "How's that plan going for ya?" knowing that the answer was going to be very clear. Not well. I proposed not reducing his plan but merely adding another element to compliment his strategy, a new arrow in the quiver. What if he looked at his addiction as a more of a choice and less of a disease? His way wasn't working, so an alternative approach couldn't hurt. I am pleased to report that in my most recent conversations (we talk often), he seems to be progressing well. I offered this as a friend, and by no means am I implying this was some medical breakthrough in any way. I am frustrated with hearing and reading about people dying, so I will do what I need to do to help. I am very intrigued by this approach and will spend time researching and learning more as I keep moving along this enlightening journey I am on. I have faith that, through projects like this book, I will inevitably meet some very educated and intelligent people that have my same outlook, and I am excited to pursue this option further.

After Seth's death, I was talking to Ian and trying to come up with a golf-related metaphor to help him understand addiction. I said, "Ian, you know the best way to become a great sand trap (bunker) player?" Ian hesitated, thinking he was going to tell me something I wanted to hear like more practice or use a different type of club. After his response, I said, "The best way to be a great sand trap player is don't go into the sand trap in the first place!" In other words, **"the best way to quit drugs and alcohol is never to start!"** That did resonate with him as he actually used that quote later on in one of his interviews using golf to help relate to addiction and substance abuse. **"Don't start"** became a sort of a personal slogan for us when we spoke to others.

The earlier an individual begins smoking, drinking, or using drugs, the higher likelihood they have of becoming addicted. The Center on Addiction has some alarming statistics on this:

- 9 out of 10 people who abuse or are addicted to nicotine, alcohol, or other drugs began using these substances before 18 years old.
- People who began using addictive substances before age 15 are nearly 7 times likelier to develop a substance problem than those who delay first use until age 21.
- Every year that substance abuse is delayed during the period of adolescent brain development, the risk of addiction, and substance abuse decreases.

It seems to me that there is a 'window of opportunity' for us to get to these kids before the age of 15 and have discussions (not lectures) about these issues.

Whether you believe addiction to be a choice or a disease, you'll probably be right. One model of thought today is what's called the Choice Model:

"In simple terms, the choice model of addiction contradicts the disease approach employed in 12 step treatment by stating that each individual can choose whether he or she uses drugs. While some advocates of the 12 step approach will concede that drug use is initially a choice which then develops into a brain disease, supporters of the choice model refuse to accept that a disease has anything to do with addiction at all. They believe that choices were made to start using drugs, and therefore that choices can be made to stop. The debate between these two camps has raged for decades and shows no signs of abating." – addiction.com

The choice model does not look at addiction from a biological viewpoint but from your own thought process. This model does take into consideration environmental factors such as poverty. Why is this something to consider? Well, I think what you believe may very well affect how you view sobriety and, ultimately, yourself. Some addicts have fully accepted this as a disease and are more inclined to keep using it as an excuse.

Regardless of which school of thought you buy into, your own experiences and attitudes can have a significant influence on what and how you approach addictions. The mind is a very powerful tool and often can do much more than you realize. For some, it may just be mind over matter. There are often alternative ways to look at health diagnosis.

One such mental health diagnosis is Post-traumatic stress disorder (PTSD). PTSD is triggered by a terrifying event, either experiencing it or witnessing it. It can result in nightmares, flashbacks, and severe anxiety many times leading to substance abuse and addictions to numb the pain. Fortunately, most people who have experienced traumatic events do not develop PTSD. **The unexpected death of a loved one accounts for approximately 20% of PTSD cases worldwide (WHO).** Unknown to me before writing this book was the concept of Post-traumatic growth theory or PTG.

Post-traumatic growth is a theory developed by psychologists Richard Tedeschi, Ph.D., and Lawrence Calhoun, Ph.D., in the mid-1990s. The theory claims people who endure psychological struggle following adversity can see positive growth afterward. "People develop new understandings of themselves, the world they live in, how to relate to other people, the kind of future they might have, and a better understanding of how to live life," says Tedeschi. PTG can be confused with being resilient, but they are different.

I had never heard of PTG, and I would bet most of you haven't either. The key aspect of this theory is that people with PTG are typically the ones that have had trouble bouncing back from traumatic events in the past. Dr. Kanako Taku, Ph.D., associate professor of psychology at Oakland University and a survivor of the 1995 Kobe earthquake in Japan, has studied this as well. He stated, "Resilience is the personal attribute or ability to bounce back. PTG, on the other hand, refers to what can happen when someone who has difficulty bouncing back experiences a traumatic event that challenges his or her core beliefs, and then ultimately finds a sense of personal growth."

I am quite baffled that this concept isn't more popular in the mainstream media? It would seem to me that at least knowing about this may help people form a more positive approach to their plan in coping with pain and suffering, give them hope or at least a light at the end of the tunnel. In 1996 Tedeschi and Calhoun developed the Post-Traumatic Growth Inventory (PTGI) to help people evaluate to what extent someone has achieved growth after trauma. It looks for positive responses in five areas;

- Appreciation of life
- Relationships with others
- New possibilities in life
- Personal growth
- Spiritual change

The scale is being revised to add updates to spiritual change to "to incorporate more existential themes that should resonate with those more secular (non-religious)," says Tedeschi. Although a relatively newer concept, I plan to study this much more as I expand my knowledge into addictions, substance abuse, and trauma. At a minimum, people should be aware this is out there.

A National Epidemic

In the late 1990s, many pharmaceutical companies promoted the idea of opioids as non-addictive to the medical community. The rates of prescriptions of opioid medications increased substantially, which led to widespread misuse of both prescription and non-prescription opioids. It soon became apparent the early assessments to alleviate the addiction worries were baseless and not justified.

Drug overdoses ensued and have continued to rise in the United States. From 1999 to 2017, more than 702,000 people have died from a drug overdose. In 2017 alone, more than 70,000 people died from drug overdoses, of which 68% involved a prescription or illicit opioid. (Center for Disease Control and Prevention, National Center for Injury Prevention and Control-10/18/19). A month doesn't go by without a well-known individual's name being added to the list.

Here is a shortlist of just some of the more famous names since 1990:

River Phoenix	1993 (Age 23)	Cocaine & Heroin
Chris Farley	1997 (Age 33)	Cocaine & Morphine
Ike Turner	2007 (Age 76)	Cocaine
Heath Ledger	2008 (Age 28)	Multiple Opioid
Whitney Houston	2012 (Age 27)	Cocaine
Philip Seymour Hoffman	2014 (Age 46)	Multiple Drug
Tyler Sash	2015 (Age 27)	Multiple Opioid
Scott Weiland	2015 (Age 48)	Multiple Drug
Prince	2016 (Age 57)	Fentanyl
Tom Petty	2017 (Age 66)	Multiple Drug
Art Bell	2018 (Age 72)	Prescription Opioids
Mac Miller	2018 (Age 26)	Fentanyl & Cocaine
Juice WRLD	2019 (Age 21)	Oxycodone & Codeine
Chynna Rogers	2020 (Age 26)	Unknown Drug

What a powerful list from a wide breadth of talents. I hate to think of whose name will be next.

Opioids are a class of drugs used to reduce pain. Some of the popular prescription opioids are oxycodone (Oxycontin), hydrocodone (Vicodin), morphine, and methadone. Fentanyl is a synthetic pain reliever, approved for treating severe pain, typically advanced stages of cancer. Unfortunately, it is added, illegally, to heroin and cocaine to increase the potency and the users high. Synthetic opioid deaths, including fentanyl, increased by 47% from 2016 to 2017. Slightly over 28,000 people died from overdoses involving synthetic opioids, not including methadone in 2017. The statistics are staggering:

BY THE NUMBERS-THE OPIOID EPIDEMIC
From hhs.gov/opioids

- 130+ people died every day from opioid-related drug overdoses
- 47,600 people died from overdosing on opioids
- 81,000 people used heroin for the first time
- 32,656 deaths attributed to overdosing on synthetic opioids other than methadone (in the 12-month period ending February 2019)
- 10.3 million people misused prescription opioids in 2018

- 2.0 million people had an opioid disorder in 2018
- 2 million people misused prescription opioids for the first time
- 808,000 people used heroin in 2018
- 15,349 deaths attributed to overdosing on heroin (in a 12-month period ending February 2019)

The year Seth died, there were 42,000 opioid overdoses in the United States alone, more than any previous year on record. It was painfully clear we had a problem. Many of the above statistics ended with opioid overdoses, but they started with substance abuse and addiction issues, usually alcohol and marijuana.

Surprisingly, recent research seems to suggest teens are trying marijuana before alcohol and tobacco. When I first heard of this, I was quite shocked as I assumed teens started with beer, then progressed to harder liquor then marijuana. It's not because teens are consuming more pot, it's because they are using tobacco and alcohol less. Katherine M Keyes, a professor of epidemiology at Columbia University and co-author of a study published in the journal Drug and Alcohol Dependence, sees the gateway pattern of adolescent substance use is changing.

"As we've seen the dramatic declines in alcohol and tobacco, we haven't seen dramatic declines in marijuana, so now every year it's more and more likely that kids are starting their drug-use careers with marijuana," says Keyes. One important note is this data did not include the spike in underage vaping, which is becoming an issue all on its own.

In the opening paragraph of this book, I alluded to a story that greatly impacted me after I had presented to a class at Prairie High School in Cedar Rapids, Iowa. Lisa Powers was the teacher for that 9th-grade Health class in 2018. I recently reached out to her to follow up and discovered she has seen a rise in mental health issues with adolescents and has concerns with higher risk behaviors. "Trying to understand and predict high-risk behaviors in students starts as early as elementary school," she mentioned. "Vaping is becoming a very big problem, with over 100 vapes being confiscated in just one day alone last year," she added.

Vaping has become one of the most popular forms of substance abuse among adolescents today. An electronic vapor device typically allows the user to inhale and exhale ingredients such as nicotine, marijuana, and various other types of flavorings and chemicals, many of which can be toxic. The U.S. Centers for Disease Control and

Prevention (CDC) reported in 2019 that 27.5% of high school students and 10.5% of middle school students claimed to have used a vaping product in the past 30 days. That is an alarming 32% increase among high school students and an unbelievable 114% increase among middle school students, despite increased attention and education. The fact these are the most formable years for young brains to develop and are at the highest risk for addiction is very troublesome. The CDC reports teens and adults who vape are about four times as likely to end up smoking traditional cigarettes. Parents, I implore you to learn more about this topic and talk to your kids.

I thought it was encouraging the educational system is spending less time on content-based education and more on helping students as she says, "make better choices, changing behaviors and understanding the why." We both agree that positive goal setting and forming consistent, repeatable habits is vital in guiding these kids. These issues aren't unique to Cedar Rapids, Iowa.

President Donald Trump declared the opioid crisis a national public health emergency in 2017. In April 2018, Dr. Ben Carson, secretary of the U.S. Department of Housing and Urban Development (HUD), visited Cedar Rapids, Iowa, to address the opioid issue. The Area

Substance Abuse Council (ASAC) was the organization
chosen for his visit.

Meeting Dr. Ben Carson at ASAC on April 19, 2018

Formed in 1962, ASAC is a private, non-profit corporation
that seeks to provide accessible, comprehensive behavioral
health services to reduce the impact of substance abuse
disorders. Seth was a patient there for a while after high
school, and I became very familiar with the services and
benefits they provide to a community very much in need. I
went from not knowing what ASAC stood for to today,
completing my 2nd full year as a member of the ASAC
Board of Directors. As an ASAC board member and

83

parent of a child taken by drugs, I was honored to be asked to sit on a panel to discuss this important challenge. In the meeting held at the ASAC Boardroom on Thursday, April 19th, 2018, Dr. Carson commented, "We will continue to have a problem until treatment is as easy to access as the drugs." We have a long road in front of us, and the fact that a member of the President's team made the trip to Cedar Rapids shows how dire the situation must be.

Golf Saved My Life

Loss is an **event,** but grief is a *process,* as is recovery - a never-ending process. I think many people struggling with addictions and anxiety believe one day it will just go away. Go to a few meetings, read a book, or take a pill. Time heals all wounds they say. I would say time "assists in the perpetual process of healing but not in total healing itself, " as I am not sure you truly ever heal completely. It is also said wounds heal and build scar tissue. On the surface, scar tissue may look tougher than normal skin, but it is inferior to healthy skin in many ways. Beyond the obvious unpleasant appearance, it is stiffer and less pliable.

I believe a key is developing coping mechanisms and having realistic expectations **BEFORE** trauma occurs and not just try to rely on developing scar tissue after the fact. Emotional scar tissue often never heals. The "getting over it" mentality can be a fragile and a false foundation that has the potential to crumble and isn't for everyone, especially when a traumatic experience follows a traumatic experience, as occasionally it does.

Often after a devastating event, we gravitate to something to escape. Not always good, I may add, and ironically this focused attention can become an obsession or addiction itself. Addiction often has negative emotional aspects, and as we are painfully aware, it can wreak havoc on not only the addicted but those around them. Drug and alcohol abuse can increase, and the griever becomes as bad or worse than the one they are grieving. It simply doesn't have to be this way. It's your choice.

In my case, my addiction became golf, and it quickly became a more positive outlet for my grieving process than I could have ever imagined. Let me make it clear this wasn't about me becoming addicted to playing more golf. This was about me focusing on watching my middle son, Ian, pursue his dream and love for golf. Being fully present in the moment and putting my energy and focus on helping him achieve his dream of playing college golf became my "drug" of choice and boy did I consume plenty!

Golf isn't a very complicated game in itself. It's just you, a ball, and some clubs. Yet some of the world's greatest athletes have been left looking completely helpless trying to hit this dimpled, stationary object. For our family, golf and death collided on October 4, 2016, and now golf was ascending me to a higher realm of meaningful living. I used the game of golf to immerse my energy into and, at the same time, soon realized it could become a tremendous platform to do good. I found out that through immense suffering and sorrow, great things can be born!

From a very young age, Ian had an interest in most sports, but golf seemed to grab his attention. He must have been two years old when my wife bought a plastic golf set. Immediately, Ian went to the back yard to pound his new multi-colored plastic golf balls as far and as hard as he could. I came home from work one afternoon and saw him whacking balls in the backyard and looking like he was having a great time. I thought to myself, "Hey, he has a decent swing." Now, I know what you are thinking - he was only two. I know most parents watching their kids typically say the same thing. We, for the most part, are all optimistically delusional when it comes to our kids. I get it. Nonetheless, I kept getting him clubs as he grew, and we evolved from the backyard to hitting buckets of balls at the range.

Young Ian (Age 3) in the Backyard With His Plastic Golf Set

The range we went to most often at that young age was the
Airport National Golf complex in Cedar Rapids, Iowa. Mark
Lemon was the owner at the time, and he was very helpful
to Ian in some of his early lessons. Matt Erger is the current
proprietor and has been super in letting us use his facilities.
Airport National is the home course for the Prairie High
School Golf team that Ian would eventually play for.
Airport National is a very short, par 62 course, with
deceptively undulating, evil greens. Many kids come out to
Airport National thinking they are going to shoot -7 under
par and end up leaving frustrated. It's aptly named as
airplanes fly over the course all day coming and going from
The Cedar Rapids Municipal Airport.

In 2006, we decided to join Elmcrest Country Club in Cedar Rapids, Iowa. Seth was thirteen, Ian was five, and Roman was three. We thought it would be an excellent investment for Ian's golf career. Also, the business contacts for my growing wealth management firm, Premier Investments of Iowa, Inc., would be greatly enhanced. Kind of the proverbial killing two birds with one stone. I founded the company at age twenty-three and increasing our presence in the business community certainly couldn't hurt. However, the real reason we joined was Larry Gladson.

Ian (Age 5) Golfing at Elmcrest

Larry was, and as I write this, still is the head pro at the club. Elmcrest CC was founded in 1947 and has become a staple not only in Iowa but in the Midwest. The golf course isn't long, but the greens are fast and sloped, and when in full bloom, the trees can make the fairways pretty tight. It has a great feel to it, and we were very happy we joined. Ian immediately began lessons with the assistant pro, Brian Johnson, for a few years, and then Larry took over. Larry Gladson had worked with many golfers that went on to have great high school and college careers. Then in 2007, something amazing happened not only to Elmcrest CC and Cedar Rapids but to the whole state of Iowa. Local product Zach Johnson won The Masters.

I remember being in my basement and seeing Ian watch with tremendous pride as Zach, a kid from Elmcrest CC, who attended Drake University in Des Moines, IA - beat Tiger Woods and others to win the 2007 Masters. Zach had honed his skills growing up playing at Elmcrest CC and had a great high school career at Cedar Rapids Regis High School, now Cedar Rapids Xavier High School. Coincidentally the same high school that produced NFL QB Hall of Famer, Kurt Warner. Both of them have very similar stories of perseverance and being *undeterred*.

In that moment, in our basement, Ian knew that it was possible to have big dreams and to achieve them. I can't imagine how many kids in this state and the Midwest looked at that day as a turning point. The next year Zach came back to the club for a private meet and greet. We brought a few items for him to sign, and we had a photo taken with Zach and my family. Zach has raised millions of dollars through his Zach Johnson Foundation and his annual Zach Johnson Foundation Classic at Elmcrest Country Club in Cedar Rapids, Iowa.

Prudence, Seth, Me, Ian, and Zach Johnson at Elmcrest CC (2007)

The Zach Johnson Foundation was founded in 2010, to set children on a path to post-secondary success. The foundation's program, Kids on Course, sets out to address the academic achievement gap between low-income and their higher-income peers in the community, serving over 1,000 students and eight schools.

The photo with Zach ended up being important to us as Seth was there that day, along with my wife and Ian. As it turned out a few years later, Zach would be an important part of our story, and we will forever remain grateful for his support and help in bringing awareness to substance abuse and addiction issues.

Ian entered his first golf tournament shortly after we joined Elmcrest, with most events being 2-5 holes. He won a few early on and then had a few that didn't turn out so well. Around eight years old, he started playing on the Iowa Junior Golf Tour (PGA Iowa Section) and what was then The Plantations Tour. The Plantations Tour was eventually sold to the Hurricane Junior Golf Tour (HJGT), which has become one of the most respected Junior Golf Tours available. In 2017, the NEXUS Group became a lead partner in the HJGT with Tiger Woods and Justin Timberlake getting involved. Ian continued playing tournaments across the country and began making a name for himself in the junior golf world.

Ian (Age 11) with his first-place trophy at the Quad City Junior
Short Hills CC in East Moline, IL

I remember a time when Ian was in the seventh grade; he
had just won a junior golf tournament out of state. I was
talking with a parent from another Cedar Rapids school,
and they had asked about which high school Ian was going
to play for. When I mentioned Prairie High School, they
kind of chuckled and said, "Ian should transfer - we'd win
State for sure!" This comment was in jest, but I will say that

wasn't the last time someone brought up the idea of transferring away from Prairie. As I mentioned before, Prairie was not a golf school. One night Ian and I were talking, and the conversation I had with this parent came up. As we spoke, I asked him, "Do you want to be part of an existing golf culture that has a chance to win every year, or do you want to be known as the person that changed the culture of the program forever? What do you want your legacy to be?"

As I mentioned before, the day of Seth's death, Ian was on his way to the District Golf Tournament. Over the course of the next few years, golf became more than just a game for our family. The golf course became a place of solace and reflection for me. I was so fortunate to be outside, walking 4-5 hours at a time, fully immersing myself in helping Ian chase his dream. **Undeterred.**

The Journey Begins

Five days after Seth passed, one of us (most likely not me as I didn't know much about this stuff) suggested we set up a GoFundMe account to raise money for something positive in Seth's honor. We agreed to raise money and donate, in Seth's memory, to The Area Substance Abuse Council (ASAC) in Cedar Rapids, Iowa, where, as I mentioned previously, Seth was a patient.

That initial idea was what really catapulted us to an amazing journey that I have the honor to write about now in this book. From the depths of misery, chaos, and despair, an inspired passion that still exists today, was born. We raised over $6,000 through GoFundMe with the generous donations and contributions of friends, family, and many people we had never met.

Presenting the GoFundMe Fundraiser Check to ASAC

I recall the first time Seth went to ASAC. In 2015, three years post-high school, Seth had been told by us he could no longer stay at our house as it wasn't conducive to a positive environment for the other kids or us. There was too much lying and tension. Tough love, I guess it's called. Sounds great in theory, but dropping your teenager off downtown on a freezing cold Friday afternoon not knowing where he would go was extremely difficult. Necessary, but very hard to do, nonetheless. Until you've been there, I ask you not to judge.

Shortly afterward, Seth was hospitalized with an alcohol overdose. My wife, Roman and I were on the golf course following Ian, when I got a call that Seth was in the ER. We immediately went to the hospital and were told we could not see him. He was later put into a private room, and we once again went to see him. As we approached his room, we saw an armed guard outside his door. Seth was going through such severe withdrawals that he became unruly. At this moment, I wondered whether I should take Ian and Roman home but ultimately made the decision not to shield them from the reality of the situation. I believed this would be a valuable life lesson for both of them.

The situation had become serious, and I had absolutely no idea whom to call or ask for help. No clue. I finally looked online, and that's where I found ASAC. I called them and was told they had no beds or rooms available. Up to this point, I didn't know what they did. I just knew they took in, temporally, those who had alcohol and/or drug issues, and that was Seth. I told the lady on the phone, "my son needs a bed today, or he won't make it to Monday." I was essentially begging for him to get in. I was told there was nothing they could do. As I hung up, I looked out my office window, snow falling calmly, wondering what plan B was going to be. Or would we even make it to plan B?

It wasn't much longer than fifteen minutes, and my cell phone rang. It was ASAC. They had a bed available for Seth immediately. Someone made it happen, and for that, I will be forever grateful. ASAC went the extra mile to help Seth and us. I called my wife, told Seth the plan, and we checked him in as soon as he was released from the hospital. A few days into treatment, we received a call that they were considering removing him as he was becoming difficult and angry. I am sure coming off the drugs and alcohol was making things worse for him in the short term.

After a few days, he became a model patient. Seth graduated after thirty days at ASAC, and during that time, we visited him frequently, as did a few of his closest friends. Justin Gill was Seth's best friend, and he was always there for Seth. Justin seemed to be a good influence on Seth and was one friend that was there for him at all times. One of my proudest moments with Seth was graduation day at ASAC, even more than his high school graduation day oddly enough.

At his ASAC graduation ceremony, we sat in a large circle with the other patients and their loved ones. In our case, it was me, my wife, Ian, and Roman. As we went around the room, each one of us got to speak about whatever we wanted to talk about. Seth commented on how he was proud of himself for seeking treatment and thanked us for our patience. We all cried and listened as each patient talked about their struggles and thanked those loved ones who stood by them. It was a very inspiring day for me.

Hugging and sharing tears with complete strangers was one of the most humbling moments of my life. No successful stock investment or amount of money can even come close to what I felt that day. I often wonder how many of the graduates that day made it back to ASAC as repeaters or how many ended up like our son? At that time, according to ASAC, about sixty percent of the patients were able to meet their treatment goals. Unfortunately, this also meant forty percent ended back in treatment.

Soon after the GoFundMe ran its course, Ian began asking what else we could do. We wanted to continue with the momentum we had going to keep raising awareness and funds. It was at that time I recalled a program through the American Junior Golf Association (AJGA) called Leadership Links. It was the brainchild of the AJGA, specifically Beth Dockter. Leadership Links allows junior golfers throughout the world to raise money through golf to benefit a charity or organization of their choosing. I went to their website and emailed them to get more information. Looking back, I am so happy I did.

I received an email from Beth, and we established an account for Ian. Essentially, Ian could accept donations directly, or people could pledge money for each birdie he had during the season. At the end of the season, the proceeds raised would be split evenly between ASAC and the AJGA's ACE Grant program which assists Junior golfers to enter events that do not have the financial resources to do so. As you can imagine, golf is an expensive sport for many families, and it's unfortunate when young golfers can't play and compete simply because they are priced out. The AJGA has hit a hole in one with Leadership Links. Golf clap.

During the Summer of 2017, Ian played in several events. As he headed into his junior year of high school, he was starting to get some local media attention about his desire to honor his brother and those affected by substance abuse. It had only been nine months since losing Seth. At times, the added attention reopened raw feelings and emotions. As we all know, grieving is processed differently for everyone, and during this time, it was difficult to focus on that along with helping Ian. I had Roman to keep an eye on making sure he felt involved in this project that we, as a family, had embarked on. Roman had thrown himself into wrestling and getting heavy into music and singing.

I recall a lighthearted moment in 2017 while Roman was in the midst of his 7th grade wrestling season. Ian wanted to honor Seth by pointing his putter to the sky after each birdie, and Roman came up with the idea of pointing to the sky after each pin. After one hard-fought overtime win, Roman went to the middle of the mat to shake hands with his dejected opponent. He then proudly and triumphantly pointed to the sky in honor of Seth. Immediately the referee, thinking Roman was claiming to be #1 and bragging, told him not to do that as it was poor sportsmanship. As Roman came off the mat, puzzled, he looked to me as if he were in trouble. I smiled and told him it was a simple misunderstanding, and after explaining to the official, all was well. Life has its funny moments, even during tough times.

Roman's Freshman Year Wrestling Photo

That August, a local sportswriter for The Cedar Rapids Gazette, K.J. Pilcher, called me at our home one evening wanting to talk. He had heard about Ian's desire to use golf to raise awareness and money to honor Seth. That evening K.J. did a phone interview with Ian, and as far as I knew, it went well. Ian didn't say a whole lot, and like most teenagers, often resigned to one-word sentences. I didn't think much more about the interview at the time.

Ian started his junior year with a ton of momentum and challenges. Between his sophomore and junior years, he grew an incredible nine inches. For most sports, that's a great competitive advantage, but for golf, it can be devastating. He stood now slightly over 6' 3" and, unknown to him, had another 2 inches to go before graduation.

The morning of August 10th, 2017 was Ian's first high school tournament his junior year. As we headed out to Ellis Golf Course in Cedar Rapids, I stopped by a local gas station to grab a coffee. I picked up the local newspaper, The Cedar Rapids Gazette, and headed out to the course. I tossed it into the back seat, thinking nothing in the paper that day would probably be of much interest. Man, was I wrong.

As I headed to the clubhouse, I had a ton of parents and players stop me to say that we were doing a great job, and they were thinking of us and our plight. I thought it was kind of strange as it was pretty much everyone I ran into. I even had kids and coaches wanting to give me cash donations! It was then that a parent handed me the front section of the sports page of the Gazette, and there it was, a picture of Ian and the headline "*Brother's death motivates Prairie golfer Ian Johnston to help those battling addiction.*" Wow.

I started to cry as I realized that even with everything we had been through, we were beginning to make a difference. An eerie sentence in K.J's article was soon to have an unforeseen and uncanny accuracy. Towards the end of the article, K.J writes, "Johnston admitted it would be nice to clinch a state berth with a birdie, serving as another tribute to his late brother." K.J has since been a tremendous resource and supporter of our cause, and I am forever grateful for him reaching out to us that evening. Ian ended up shooting an even par 72, finishing runner-up in what was to be the start of an amazing year.

Golfing With Purpose

After the article in the Cedar Rapids Gazette, momentum began to pick up significantly, and we were presented with new opportunities, through golf, to share our story and raise awareness for substance abuse and addictions.

We started to get donations into Ian's Leadership Links account at the AJGA along with social media starting to help spread the story. Soon after this, Cody Goodwin, a sportswriter from The Des Moines Register, reached out, had heard our story, and wanted to meet Ian but, more importantly, our family. We met Cody at Airport National Golf course after Ian finished practice one beautiful Fall afternoon.

I remember the time and effort Cody took when preparing the story, and he was very attentive to every detail we could provide him. Cody had tipped us off that the Des Moines Register was running the story on Sept 27, 2017, two days after what would have been Seth's 24th birthday and almost a year since his death. The past year had felt like a hundred years and also like a hundred hours all at the same time.

"This one's for you... Opioids killed his brother. A top Iowa golfer now strives to honor his memory." This was the cover story that day at The Des Moines Register. Not the sports section but the *entire* front page. I was not sure up to this point how important telling our story was until I realized how many families and lives were impacted by the story that day. The Des Moines Register has an extensive reach. The article was very well written and, at times, was tough to read. Cody really touched the essence and pain that goes with losing a loved one to addiction. Again, our thanks go out to Cody Goodwin and The Des Moines Register for helping us gain even more momentum and awareness on what was becoming a national epidemic.

The Iowa Department of Public Health released a state report showing that the number of in-state opioid overdoses jumped from 28 in 2005 to 67 in 2016 and that opioid-related (non-overdose) deaths climbed from 59 in 2005 to 146 last year. Over a hundred people a day died nationwide during this time. According to ASAC, 84% of all overdose incidents in Iowa in 2015 involved heroin or other opioid drugs. A year later, that number had ballooned to more than 800. Around this time, I noticed a tremendous amount of national attention committed to this issue.

A few weeks before the Cedar Rapids Gazette article ran, a popular TV golf host announced his son had passed from an overdose. At the time, NBC Sports and Golf Channel personality, David Feherty, revealed his son, Shey, had died on July 29th, 2017, his 29th Birthday. "Shey fought hard to win his battle with drug addiction and mental illness, but in the end, the monsters won" Feherty, so impassionedly tweeted out on August 1st, 2017. I was just starting to get more fuel added to the already simmering fire inside me. It was beginning to seem like every week someone in the national spotlight was choked by the hand of this insidious beast.

The people we have met through golf have been amazing. One standout individual we met on Ian's junior golf tour was Paul Ellis. Paul had worked for the Plantations Tour for over two decades and is one of those rare people you meet with a genuinely positive attitude. I can count the people on one hand that I have met in my life that are that way. He was always trying to cheer the players (and us parents!) up after tough rounds and the first to congratulate them when they succeeded. He welcomed us into his home on more than one occasion. Paul has the unique ability to find the good in everyone and the great in living life. We need more people like Paul on this planet.

Ian and Paul Ellis at Hurricane Junior Golf Tour November 2018
Aberdeen Golf Club, Eureka, MO

It wasn't until a few years after we met that I learned he lost his daughter, Lyndsey, to Scleroderma at a young age a few years back. Paul's story is another example of persevering through something despite setbacks or, as I like to say, being *undeterred*. I reached out to Paul recently to gain a better perspective of his journey and what he is doing to raise awareness for this rare disease. A positive byproduct of writing this book is the additional knowledge I am gaining on many important topics that I wouldn't have otherwise been drawn to.

Scleroderma, I discovered, is a chronic connective tissue disease generally classified as one of the autoimmune rheumatic diseases. Less than 300,000 cases per year are reported in the US, treatment can help, but there is no cure. The disease can vary from patient-to-patient and is not contagious, infectious, or cancerous.

Lyndsey was diagnosed at 15 years old, and to this day, they do not know how she got the disease. That summer, she had come home from a camp and had mentioned something "felt weird." The exact cause or causes of scleroderma are still unknown, but medical researchers and scientists are making strides in making those determinations. What we do know is scleroderma involves an overproduction of collagen with female patients outnumbering male patients 4-to-1.

Paul explained to me she had systemic sclerosis, which indicates a (hardening) may occur in the internal systems of the body. After her senior year in high school, she had a stem cell transplant and, with additional therapy, was feeling better as she headed off to attend William Woods University in Fulton, MO. Ten days later, on August 29th, 2010, her "heart just gave out," as Paul described to me in a soft voice, "She was only 19 years old."

This year marked the 10th annual Lyndsey Ellis Memorial Basketball Tournament. It is a great event that raises money and awareness in St. Louis and surrounding areas where Paul and his family reside. Proceeds go to a number of different entities, one being the Missouri Chapter of the Scleroderma Foundation at www.scleroderma.org. Paul has been active in education and raising awareness of this issue.

Bob Saget, best known for his role on the TV sitcom, Full House, and America's Funniest Home Videos, lost his sister, Gay, to this disease. She was diagnosed in 1992 at the age of 44 and died two years later at 46 years old. Mr. Saget is a Scleroderma Research Foundation board member and active advocate for this affliction.

I think it's interesting and so accurate how Paul identified his two sons, PJ and Ryan, as "keeping him alive" during this ordeal as I have said the same thing many times about Ian and Roman. Family, friends, and relationships do so much to help those with not only the trauma endured, but the impending sorrow and grief to follow.

Paul, I am honored to call you a friend, and thank you for making the people around you better. Keep raising awareness and funds to fight the disease that took your beloved daughter!

We began traveling with another youth golfer and his dad to save travel expenses. The miles we have driven with Brian Barnhart and his son, Brock, are immeasurable. We would go to Chicago and St Louis and so many other cities, which seemed like a few times per month. It was always a fun "weekend getaway," and it was an excellent experience for Ian as Brock was and is a very accomplished youth golfer that pushed Ian to get better. We consoled each other many times after tough events and proudly smiled when they won. I am very grateful for those moments and even as stressful as they were at times, I do miss them dearly.

Vindication

It's rare to have High School Golf Districts at the same course in back to back years, yet there it was, Pheasant Ridge Golf Course was to be the location of Districts in early October 2017. I had mixed emotions as this was precisely where, a year earlier, our lives took a huge detour. Ian had missed State two years in a row on the last hole each time, and now his junior year, we were going back to the place where this all began. Fate or Curse?

I circled the date on my calendar, and we anxiously prepared for the inevitable return in early October 2017. This was either going to be an opportunity for vindication for Ian on the course near where his brother died a year prior, or it was going to add to our already painful experiences. Moments like these are precisely why athletes love to compete and be in these situations. "After all, he needs to put on a show. His older brother will be watching" was the last sentence in Cody Goodwin's story in the Des Moines Register. How accurate that statement was to be.

The day came, and I made a very tough decision. With the added media attention building up and the fact I knew a local TV station would be following Ian, I decided to stay home. I believed my presence could only hurt him, and I was going to do anything I could to help him, even if that meant staying home. Looking back now, I anguished a bit not going, but at the same time, I try not to live in a world of regret and hindsight for very long. My wife headed up that day, and I stayed home going crazy, wondering how the team was doing. To say it was tortuous would be an understatement. After a few hours of slamming coffees, I actually fell asleep in my chair watching TV.

I awoke with the sound of my phone vibrating, and I noticed I had a bunch of new texts. Reluctantly, one eye closed, I took a peek not sure what to expect. I was either going to be very pleased, or disappointment would ensue. I remember seeing a picture of the team holding a 2017 State Qualifier Flag and a text from Ian "**DAD WE MADE STATE!!!.**" First time in school history! WOW! I fell to my knees, letting out a massive scream of pent up frustrations and a complete release of emotions. It was one of the greatest moments of my life. I want to believe Seth, wherever he was, he was smiling that day for his little brother, for all of us. As I was to find out, the drama that had unfolded on the last hole was something scripted only in a movie.

Prairie Golf October 2017
Left to Right: Zach Zahner, Sam Lockhart, Griffin Clark, Ian Johnston,
Jeremy Jennissen, Jared Tjelmeland, Coach Erik Columbus

A few weeks prior, sports reporter Zach Hanley with local TV Channel 2 KGAN, a CBS affiliate, had done a great feature on Ian and his golf journey. He captured so much in his story, and I have to be honest, have watched it too many times to count. Matt Lange, a cameraman for KGAN drove up to Districts to report on the local golfers but had his eye on the young man Zach had interviewed a short while back. Not being present at the tourney, I can only repeat what people had told me about that day.

The day was back and forth with our conference rival Lin-Mar being the team that was most likely to ruin our day. They have a rich tradition of State golf history and were, by all means, the favorite to get the last qualifying spot, definitely over Prairie, a school not known for golf. They had had a roster full of very talented seniors that had qualified for the State tourney the year prior.

Understand that golf is a team game, and every single one of the players for Prairie had an equal hand in getting them to State. No "one" shot was any more important than another. Nonetheless, it fittingly came down to the last hole. Hole #18 at Pheasant Ridge is a short par 4 that you cannot hit long over the pin on your approach shot. It's a 380-yard slight dogleg right, very typical golf hole you'd see at many courses in Iowa. Any putt above the hole was ghoulishly difficult as it was super-fast and had a very wicked break. Let me reiterate; DON'T GO LONG. As Coach Columbus later added, "Just two-putting from there would have been great, I saw a few three putts from that same spot." Ian hit, of course, his approach long, over the pin. He had an approximate 18 foot very difficult downhill birdie attempt. Channel 2 cameraman Matt Lange moved around the green positioning himself, the camera on his shoulder trying to get the best shot of Ian's putt.

Unknown to everyone, Lin Mar and Prairie were tied for the last spot. One team advances the next week to play in Marshalltown, Iowa, at Elmwood CC for a chance at State; the other team goes home. I can only imagine the specter of Ian's previous disappointments at Districts loomed over him. This hole was the scene of last year's late-round carnage and was only a few miles from where his older brother Seth had passed the previous year during Districts. As I said, Hollywood couldn't have scripted this opportunity any better for Ian. No one knew at the time that even if Ian two putts for par, Lin-Mar would beat Prairie on a card-back to go to State. Card backs are often used in lieu of a playoff in golf to settle a tie and can vary in method. Make the putt, and it wouldn't matter.

I am so grateful Channel 2 was present, and we will forever have the video of that putt. As the lanky lefty stroked the ball towards the hole, the putt started out to Ian's left and headed downhill. The ball bounced slightly as it began its journey helped along by gravity. It starts to break to the right as if guided by an invisible hand towards the cup. It can't go in, can it? Will this be Ian's vindication and a moment for us to cherish as we cope with the grief this same day a year ago so provided us? As the ball disappears into the cup for birdie, an enormous smile breaks over Ian's face. As he had done all year, he picked the ball up, pointed his putter to the sky, and thought to himself, "*This one's for you, Seth.*" Like I said, amazing how that day unfolded for us and all those with the Prairie Golf program.

Ian Pointing His Putter To The Sky For Seth After Making The Putt That Got Prairie to The State Tournament

Impermanence: Every experience comes to an end. I didn't want this day to end. We don't quite live as if that were the case as we continually surrender to the illusion we will soon arrive at some final destination. We get to what we believe is that time, yet we are unprepared to enjoy it. Well, for us, this was a moment we wanted to hold onto forever yet well knowing its life span was limited. "**Enjoy the moment**" became our new mantra.

Ian has missed plenty of putts over his young career from that distance, but not this time. Ian could have chosen alcohol and drugs to numb his pain, but he chose golf. For that moment, golf had chosen us, and I am very grateful to have shared that moment, even from the confines of my living room, while jumping up and down!

The 2017 Class 4A State Golf Participant Prairie High School
Front Row (L-R): *Jeremy Jennissen, Sam Lockhart, Griff Clark, Coach Tyler Comisky.*
Back Row (L-R): *Coach Erik Columbus, Ian Johnston, Jared Tjelmeland, Zack Zahner*

Prairie High School would end up finishing 10th place at State in 2017, and although the weather was absolutely abysmal, Ian ended up 12th individually and recorded the 3rd lowest round day 2 with a 71. Since 2016, Ian's sophomore year, Prairie has sent five boys to play collegiate golf, by far the most ever in a three-year span. The golf culture had changed. No one could deny the fact that Prairie **was** a golf school now.

I asked Ian later that night if he remembered what I told him when we were asked about transferring to another school when he was in 7th grade? He said, "yep." I said, "doesn't it feel better knowing you had a hand in changing the culture at a program rather than being a part of something already present?" As Ian looked up and smiled and said in a way, only Ian could, "yep!"

On A Roll

The Summer and Fall of 2018 were a surreal time for us. We were very active in raising awareness for substance abuse and addiction issues and trying to get Ian in front of as many college coaches as possible. To say the whole recruiting process was fun, I would be lying. I could, and may someday, write a book just on the topic of Junior Golf. I did use this opportunity to share our story with coaches and parents as we talked during rounds that Ian competed. Again, every single time I told our story, I was stunned by how many people, like us, knew or had been through substance abuse, addiction, or even mental health issues.

The first memorable event was Ian winning the Iowa Junior Amateur that Summer at Coldwater Links in Ames, Iowa. Wow, that was special and something we will always cherish. He shot 68,69 to win by 1, again in dramatic form on a 15-foot uphill putt on the last hole but this time for par.

Sadly, this was to become the course where beloved collegiate golfer Celia Barquín Arozamena was brutally murdered on September 17th, 2018. She played golf at Iowa State University and was the 2018 Big 12 Conference Champion along with being named Iowa State's Female

Athlete of The Year. I often think of how that course provided such great memories for us, yet for the Iowa State and Barquín Arozamena families, the same course must hold a completely different feeling. Ian has a yellow ribbon still attached to his golf bag we received at a golf event in honor of Celia Barquín Arozamena. Although her convicted killer, who will remain nameless here, never fully explained a motive, he did suffer from a familiar pattern. Ames police reports show he struggled with drug and alcohol abuse, mental health issues, and had an extensive criminal past as well as a dependence on methamphetamines. How senseless and tragic her death was.

In July, we headed down to play in the UHY LLP AJGA Junior Boys Championships in Eureka, Missouri. AJGA events are regarded as some of the most competitive events in Junior Golf. Many of the current PGA and LPGA players have had success on the AJGA Tour as Junior Golfers. The AJGA events usually field the best players in the country and even the world as foreign golfers make up a fair percentage of players. Just to get into an event is tough as you have to accumulate "stars" to play. The best Ian had ever finished prior was a top 25 the previous year. Little did we know how important the AJGA was going to be to us.

On the way down, Ian received an offer from the University of South Dakota, and he accepted. USD is a solid D1 golf program less than five hours from Cedar Rapids in Vermillion, South Dakota. They were interested in Ian not just as a golfer but for what he was doing outside of golf. Ian had visited a number of reputable golf programs during the recruiting process. South Dakota stood out and felt like home to him. Coach John Vining made him feel at ease and, in a way, reminded us of Coach Erik Columbus, Ian's high school golf coach. I think the pressure of college golf recruiting being lifted off of Ian gave him a new sense of calm as we prepared for the event.

Day 1 Ian started +3 after five holes, and we figured it was probably going to be just another up and down tourney. But something happened. Ian went -6 the rest of the day and finished -3 (69) overall and was in 1st place. Ian had won many junior tournaments, but this was rare territory for him at a three-day grueling AJGA event. After the round, Ian was pulled aside and interviewed by a local TV station, KSDK, they had heard about his journey using golf to do something good. It was just an added benefit to be leading the tournament. The feature played that night on local tv and Ian, and I watched it in the hotel over pizza and snacks. I told him, "Ian, you may not win, but what you are doing is winning for me." I was so proud of him. We all were so proud.

Ian's KSDK Interview July 2018

The next day was a solid -2 (70), and he pushed his lead up to 5. He played error-free and very relaxed. We headed back to the hotel room to get ready to go out to eat with Brian and Brock Barnhart like we always did. Later on, the reality settled in, "Hey, we got a chance, heck more than a chance this is his to win!" We enjoyed a nice dinner and went to bed early.

Ian started off the final round with a birdie, but his playing partner did as well. The kid was a few years younger than Ian and was from Texas. He was very good. I am sure he ended up committing to a very good D1 school. On hole #6 Ian hit his ball into a hazard and had his first double bogey of the tournament. The next hole into the hazard again off the tee but scrambled for a great bogie. It didn't help that the other kid went -1 those two holes and Ian went +3. What was a nice lead was shrinking fast.

It all changed when Ian stuck a five iron on a long par 3 over water to 5 feet and made birdie. He eagled the next hole, and I thought this is actually going to happen. AJGA events offer "live scoring," so parents and coaches can see scores in real-time. I have always made a habit to never look during a round, and this hasn't changed. I knew Ian had a great shot, but I figured some kid "carrer'd it" as we say, so I just watched him play and never looked, completely immersing myself in the moment.

I recall sitting on my portable folding golf chair up by the 18th green with the other parents as Ian hit his tee shot in the bunker on the long uphill #18 at The Legends Country Club in Eureka, MO. The Legends CC is a Robert Trent Jones, Sr. designed course tipped out at over 7,000 yards. It's a super midwestern course offering up a little of everything in its layout.

At that point, Brian Barnhart had come up to me and said, "congrats, man, looks like the boy has it won!" It was then I looked at the scores, and he had a six-shot lead! Another good family friend and Cedar Rapids golfer Conner Neighbors was playing in the event, and his father, Clark, was up by the green as well and gave me a big thumbs up.

Ian and I after he won the 2018 UHY LLP AJGA Junior Boy Championships in Eureka, MO

As Ian came up the fairway, I absolutely lost it. I cried and cried and cried, letting out so much I had been holding in. After Ian tapped in for a +2 (74) and a five-shot win, he was an AJGA Champion! Brian, very emotional as well, gave me a great, genuine man-hug, and he too was moved to tears. They had been a part of our journey as well, and

Brock had been interviewed many times about Ian and what had happened. I could see his happiness was authentic. The golf community is awesome, and that moment was the best moment I had ever witnessed in my life on a golf course. Even better than my three, yes, Ian, three holes in one! The Legends Country Club will always have a very special meaning for us. I look forward to traveling back down to play it with him soon.

As Ian received his red AJGA Champions Bag, he immediately removed Seth's bandana from his golf bag, and proudly tied it in a knot on his new bag. It was the very first thing he did.

Ian's AGJA Champions Bag with Seth's Bandana

The way home was very gratifying, and we relished in his victory together. For that moment, every single bad round, bad shot, or bad memory was extinguished. Believe it or not, that Summer got even better. He ended up winning a total of 7 times in 5 different states on three different tours. He had an absolute monster summer on the course, but what he was doing off was more impressive to me.

Gaining National Attention

About six months after the State Tournament as things
were settling down for us, I received an email from a Blake
Berson with the CBS Sports Network. Mr. Berson, a 14-
year veteran of doing sports documentaries, was surfing the
internet trying to find an inspirational story with a sports
angle. The fact he hadn't done too many golf stories, and
he is a self-proclaimed "golf nut" gave Ian's story some
initial appeal. After a few phone calls, Blake decided to
bring a member of his crew and himself out to Iowa to dive
deeper into Ian and his cause. Blake was very interested in
the rise of the opioid epidemic and even the emphasis on
fentanyl. As he said to me at one point, "Opioids don't
discriminate, this type of story needs to be heard."

They spent three days in Iowa following us around and
taping all sorts of different perspectives so people could
really see the depth of how one family was dealing with the
substance abuse issue, specifically the loss of a loved one. A
trip to ASAC ensued to see the facility and talk to those
that were there when Seth was a patient. We took a
moment to see the waiting room for ASAC patients with
Seth's picture and plaque on the wall. The waiting room
furniture and new paint were some of the beneficiaries of

that original $6,000 check donated from the go-fund-me site so many months ago.

Seth's Plaque at ASAC

I turned to look at a few of the young, teenage patients sitting there anxiously waiting to get help and fell back to a time when I imagine Seth was sitting there just like them— scared, nervous, and frustrated. I wanted to say something, but I didn't. I had a warm feeling inside that Seth was honored that way, yet I realized the depth of how I truly missed and loved him.

Amana Colonies Golf Course in Amana, Iowa, was gracious enough to block off a few holes for us so we could tape uninterrupted. Thank you, Steve Kahler, for your generosity in allowing us to use your facilities to get this done! Ian rounded up a few of his golf friends, Brock Barnhart and Conner Neighbors, to help recreate a typical golf day for Ian. Ian, Brock, and Conner went to different high schools, but all three were members of Elmcrest CC in Cedar Rapids, IA, and not surprisingly, had Larry Gladson as their swing coach. They had become great friends pushing each other to get better at golf and helping one another with life's challenges. All three of them later became First Team All-State golfers and all signed with D1 golf programs with Brock going to Iowa State in Ames, Iowa, and Conner signing with Southern Illinois University in Edwardsville, Illinois. The golf community was always there for us.

Ian Filming at Amana Colonies Golf Course June 2018 with CBS Sports
Network Film Crew along with Conner Neighbors and Brock Barnhart

As we were wrapping up the taping, which he was planning
to air in a few weeks, I mentioned to Blake the Elmcrest
connection and Zach Johnson. Maybe, just maybe he could
reach out to Zach and see if he could somehow add his
name to the story. Getting Zach to help in any would-be

great yet, I knew it was probably impossible. However, you never know until you ask.

Ian being interviewed at home by Blake Berson for the
CBS Sports Network story

Roman, at home, filming the CBS Sports Network story

As Elmcrest CC pro, Larry Gladson, later alluded to me, these individuals (pro athletes and celebrities) live in a different world. Especially the level of Zach Johnson, who had 12 PGA victories with two majors, the 2007 Masters and 2017 The Open Championship along with numerous Ryder Cup appearances. Their time is very valuable, and to get them involved in these things takes patience and respect if they are unable to commit. Athletes at that high level are bombarded with all sorts of charity and money-raising ventures.

As it turned out, at the last minute, Zach Johnson agreed to meet with Blake and his crew at the hotel Zach was staying in preparation for an upcoming event. The 2018 FedEx Playoffs were concluding, and it just so happened Zach was to play in The Northern Trust, formally The Barclays near where Blake lived in New Jersey. Fate has a remarkable way of working out in some situations. Blake commented that Zach couldn't have been nicer and went out of his way to accommodate him. If that doesn't say a lot about Zach's character, what would?

Zach took the time the night before a tournament to lend his voice to this story. I am still amazed by his gratitude and grace to do this for us. We were so grateful Zach was going to take the time to help us spread the word of substance abuse and addiction along with how sports, specifically golf, can do so much good. I am convinced people from Iowa are very special indeed, and Zach Johnson will always have a loyal following from our family. Zach has been very involved in charity and started The Zach Johnson Foundation which is dedicated to helping children and their families in Cedar Rapids.

In August of 2020, Zach Johnson was awarded the PGA Tour's Payne Stewart Award. The prestigious Payne Stewart Award is presented annually by the PGA Tour to a professional golfer who best exemplifies Stewart's steadfast values of character, charity, and sportsmanship.

Zach, from all of us, thank you for all you do!

A short time afterward, Blake sent me a finished link to the story. To say I had a flood of emotions would not do justice in how I felt. Zach Johnson narrated the nine-minute piece which ran on September 4th, 2018, approaching the second anniversary of Seth's death. Immediately the emails and texts came in from around the nation with so much support and encouragement for what we were doing. Twenty-five thousand hits in a few weeks and as of last check almost sixty-four thousand hits. The link to the story, along with other videos and articles, can be found at the end of this book. Amazing what social media can do in a positive manner in such a short time frame. The story has been replayed at many speaking engagements I have given, and I am sure many more.

Thank you, Blake Berson, you will always be considered a friend of mine.

From K.J. Pilcher, Cody Goodwin, Zach Hanley, Blake Berson, Larry Gladson, and Zach Johnson, the story of a family in the middle of the heartland in the face of adversity was resonating with thousands of people. For me, it was allowing us the opportunity to keep doing what we were doing and appreciating the road we were traveling. *Undeterred.*

Leadership Links

The American Junior Golf Association (AJGA) was started in 1978 by offering a competitive tournament environment for junior golfers. In the late '80s and early '90s with the vision of Stephen Hamblin, the AJGA began to focus and include opportunities for women and minority junior golfers. The AJGA has since grown into arguably the largest most respected Junior Golf association in The United States and throughout the globe. PGA players such as Ricky Fowler, Brandt Snedeker, Justin Thomas, and Patrick Reed honed their junior talents on the tour as well as LPGA players Morgan Pressel, Paula Creamer, Stacey Lewis, and Brittany Lincicome.

In 2009 the Leadership Links program began with around 50 junior golfers participating raising over $50,000. Beth Dockter, with the AJGA for 21 years, says, "Leadership Links gave junior golfers a platform to raise money and awareness for causes close to their hearts." She was there from the beginning and has been credited with making Leadership Links what it is today. Over $3 million dollars collectively has been raised with over 3,200 junior golfers from around the world participating. In 2003 the Achieving Competitive Excellence or ACE Grant program was added to assist those junior golfers without the resources to play in events.

Ian had joined the Leadership Links program raising money and awareness to support ASAC and also the ACE Grant program, which was a 50% beneficiary of the program. I always thought this was a great idea and really has done so much in teaching junior golfers charity and goodwill. Ian had raised a fair sum of money by the Summer of 2018, and we were doing our best to continue with our story.

Presenting the Leadership Links Check to ASAC

Ian finished up the year in fourth place, raising over $13,000 overall with Leadership Links in raising funds, and with that, he got a special treat. Ian, along with a few other top participants, got the opportunity to golf with Rickie Fowler at one of his courses near Jupiter, Florida. It was a very special day when we all flew to Florida to watch Ian play golf with Rickie Fowler. A day we will never forget, and again we are very grateful for the opportunity afforded us by the AJGA. We applaud Rickie Fowler for his continued support of the AJGA, specifically Leadership Links. Ironically later that summer, Ian, Brock, and Conner had the opportunity to play golf with Zach Johnson when he made it back to Elmcrest as he often does. Ian got to play golf with Rickie Fowler and Zach Johnson in the same year. I would say a pretty fortunate kid, indeed!

Ian and Rickie Fowler in November 2017

At one point during that day in Florida, I began conversing with an older couple on a golf cart. They had been involved with this event each year as local volunteers, and they were very inquisitive about how we ended up in this event. More

141

specifically, they were interested in what was our story? It was as if they already knew but just wanted to speak with someone.

I proceeded to tell them a short version of our story and concluded with telling them our son, Seth, had passed away from a heroin overdose in 2016. They seemed a bit put back, and as we parted ways, I didn't think much of the encounter.

On the 4th hole of the day, as I was enjoying Ian and Rickie taking turns hitting shots, I caught a glimpse of that same couple speeding up to me in their golf cart. I immediately assumed I had said something that offended them or something else. What they proceeded to tell me was that their grandchild had recently died of an overdose, and they had a hard time telling people it was heroin. Just saying heroin was tough to do for them. For me to say it so easily, they were curious if I had a tough time doing so? Was I embarrassed it was heroin?

It was like the stigma with the word heroin had such a bad connotation they were struggling with coming to terms discussing with others. I think it was possibly a generational issue as the older generation had a tougher time with this and was more likely to feel shame. Situations like this give me motivation and appreciation to keep telling our story and raising awareness that substance abuse and addiction don't need to live in the shadows anymore. I told them there was no shame in saying it was heroin. The only shame I can think of would be denying other people the opportunity to hear our story. That was not going to happen on my watch.

Leadership Links had introduced us to many successful stories of tragedy and triumph, but no story for me had a larger impact than Sam Gerry. I met Sam, now 18, in 2018, after Ian had signed up with his Leadership Links account through the AJGA. I had heard of this young man who had decided to discuss his battles with depression, suicidal thoughts, and mental health issues publicly, and I realized I had to reach out to him. Sam was very gracious and quite fearless in sharing his experiences with me in the hope they could help someone else with these very sensitive issues.

Millions of people are affected by mental illness each year in the US, with the average delay between symptom onset and treatment being approximately 11 years (National Alliance on Mental Illness). 17% of youths (6-17 years) experience a mental health disorder with suicide being the 2nd leading cause of death for people ages 10-34. Unfortunately, the numbers are increasing. The overall suicide rate has increased by 31% since 2001. Substance abuse, addictions, and mental health issues are all ominously interwoven.

I remain so impressed each time I interact with Sam. The maturity and the level of awareness he has with this issue are off the charts. He is the last kid I would imagine having these kinds of thoughts, yet exactly the type of kid we need to be attentive too, the ones seemingly invincible. Sam lives in Woburn, MA, and is a senior in high school. He is committed to playing golf at Bates College in 2021, and I have no doubt he will accomplish whatever his goals and dreams become.

Sam Gerry on the Golf Course. (Photo Cred: Joe Brown Photos)

"In 8th grade," Sam said, "I was on top of the world." He was excelling in school and enjoying his own golf journey. As he says to me, "one morning, I woke up and felt off. Empty. Not a sadness, but I didn't want to play golf anymore. As time went on, I lost my passion for everything, not just golf." He was soon diagnosed with clinical depression, defined as:

"A mental health disorder characterized by persistently depressed moods or loss of interests in activities, causing significant impairments in daily life."
-Mayo clinic

Sam also developed suicidal ideation or suicidal thoughts. The range of suicidal ideation varies significantly from random thoughts to pervasive, potentially planned out scenarios. About six months after signing up for Leadership Links through the AJGA, Sam very bravely came out with his battles with depression. It wasn't long before the local and national media grabbed hold of his compelling story of which he was able to discuss his plight on the Golf Channel. Sam and Ian have both benefited from each other's infectious energies and genuine passions with respect to their unique challenges and opportunities.

Recently I became aware of a blog started by Sam under the title "Out of The Dark." Here are a few excerpts from that post. I think it's clear to say he is an amazing young man. I doubt he will fully appreciate how much he is helping others. Keep fighting, Sam!

"Something is wrong with me. I feel like I want to die again, and I don't know where or why it started. I think it has lasted for about a month now, but I am entirely unsure. I have lost motivation to do anything and everything. Should I kill myself? What do I have to live for?"
-excerpt from blog post 1/25/2020 Sam Gerry

"Three weeks ago, I almost killed myself. In days prior, I had thought about how I would have done it. Would I drink bleach that sits just feet away from my bedroom? Would I take the chef's knife in my kitchen and slit my throat? Or would I take the same belt I wear every day and hang myself, only for my parents to find my lifeless corpse in the closet?"
- excerpt from a recent speech Sam gave to his English class

I have to say the comment with the belt brought this home to me. I couldn't get the picture out of my mind of seeing

Seth's belt, lifeless on his bed in that seedy motel room on the day of his death on October 4, 2016.

Sam closed his entry with;

"I am so excited to spread my message to as many people as I can. I am working tirelessly with various administrations/officials to find solutions to problems we have never dared to tackle, and I am so proud to be able to share that experience with those I am closest to. After all, nobody should have to suffer alone. Nobody."

Trust me, Sam, you aren't alone in this battle! I will have information at the end of this book to contact Sam to provide support, seek help yourself or donate to his worthy causes.

What Sam is doing is beyond inspirational and should be a gigantic wakeup call to parents to be aware of what is going on with their kids. We both agree one key is reaching out to kids and adolescents to discuss these topics before they become an issue. The easiest way to stop or quit anything is never to start. Coping mechanisms to deal with anxiety and stress are imperative to learning to live a life with minimal distractions from substance abuse, addiction, and mental health issues. I will discuss one coping mechanism Sam and

I both use mindfulness meditation, in an upcoming chapter.

Sam, you are an impressive young man, and we are honored to walk with you during your journey. You always have a friendly ear(s) to talk to in Iowa!

Jerry Cole Sportsmanship Award

Jerry Cole, I am told, was a down to earth and a very giving gentleman from Oklahoma and was a friend and longtime Board Member of the AJGA. He proudly loved wearing his AJGA hats that he had collected over the years, which were many. It was very fitting that the recipient of The Jerry Cole Sportsmanship Award would receive a nice trophy with an AJGA hat so prominently displayed. The award has been given annually since 1978 but was renamed The Jerry Cole Sportsmanship Award in 2000.

The engraved words on the back of the trophy articulated well in saying:

"By etching his name on the AJGA Sportsmanship Award, the AJGA honors the memory of Jerry Cole as a man who lived his life being generous, kind, and supportive of family, friends, and all those who are dedicated to junior golf. This bronze replica of Jerry's favorite hat is a reminder of how proud he was of his association with the AJGA."

Recipients of this award are juniors that have some or all of the following characteristics:
- Overcome adversity off the course

- Impact others in a positive way
- Display integrity and sportsmanship in all aspects of life
- Embody the spirit of the game by seeking opportunities to give back

The recipient also earned an entry into the highly competitive Rolex Tournament of Champions golf event and is honored at the Rolex Junior-All American Awards Banquet. The Jerry Cole Sportsmanship award is arguably the most prestigious award given to a junior golfer by the AJGA annually. Although I knew it would be very tough for Ian to win this award as there were so many touching stories, I was pleased when I found out Ian was named a finalist in late 2018. The AJGA was to select one recipient of the award among both male and female nominees. One golfer, in the world, would have a compelling enough story to say they were the 2018 Jerry Cole Leadership Award recipient.

When we found out Ian had won, I was overwhelmed. This recognition was more important and more rewarding than any golf tournament he had ever won. For us, the validation that we were helping others, making a difference in lives, meant the world. It was such a tremendous honor to have him be the 2018 recipient of the AJGA Jerry Cole Sportsmanship Award. His older brother, Seth, would have been so proud of him and how he had turned all this into something positive! The fact we could continue sharing our story with more people, especially Ian's peers, was an excellent opportunity not to be wasted.

Ian's Jerry Cole Sportsmanship Award

November 18th, 2018 Ian was a keynote presenter at The Rolex Junior All-American dinner at PGA National in Palm Harbor, Florida. It's the "Greatest Night in Junior Golf," and an awesome stage to continue this journey. What an honor for Ian and our family. We had traveled on this road this far together; it was a great moment for all of us. Below is a copy of his speech he read at the awards banquet, which Ian wrote himself.

"First, I would like to thank the AJGA and Leadership Links for this tremendous honor and for providing me a platform to raise funds for a cause that has so greatly impacted my life. I am humbled to have my name among so many great past recipients and nominees of the Jerry Cole Sportsmanship Award and thank them for the passion they bring to their own worthy causes. I thank my coaches, Erik Columbus and Larry Gladson, for supporting me on and off the course. I would also like to thank Blake Berson with CBS Sports Network and Zach Johnson for the documentary that spread awareness for substance abuse. Most importantly, I want to thank my parents for teaching me that life, like golf, doesn't always go the way we want.

In 2016 there were 42,249 opioid-related deaths in the United States. That same year in Iowa, 183 people died from opioid-related overdoses. On Oct 4th, 2016, my older brother, Seth, became one of those statistics.

That day started out like any other. I was a sophomore on my High School team and was excited about our District meet that morning. When I didn't see my parents come to the course, I knew something was wrong. I finished that day with a double bogie and missed state by one shot. I was devastated. It wasn't until I got home that I realized what devastating really was. My brother Seth was found in a hotel room less than 2 miles from where I played that day; heroin took his life; he was 23.

Not too long after, I remember my dad saying to me and my younger brother, Roman, "We have two roads to go down. One of anger, hatred, and despair, or a road of hope and inspiration." I am on the second road, and I ask you to join me.

Golf has been a passion of mine since before I can even remember. Over the past two years, golf has been a platform for me to make an impact and spread awareness about substance abuse. I have shared my family story with AJGA alumni, Ricky Fowler and Zach Johnson. Through Leadership Links and other fundraising efforts, I raised more than $25,000. $6,500 of which went to the AJGA's ACE Grant Program. The rest was donated to the Area Substance Abuse Council in Cedar Rapids, a treatment program where my brother spent time before his passing.

Last October, exactly one year from Seth's death, my high school golf team played again at the same course where we played last year. This time, I birdied the final hole to get to our State Tournament by one stroke. I believe Seth was there alongside me. I will continue to spread awareness and use golf to make an impact as I go to college and play golf at the University of South Dakota.

This room is full of great golfers with great accomplishments. I applaud all of you. However, please remember you also have a tremendous opportunity to use golf to create great change in the world. Trophies gather dust, but making an impact in the lives of others will last forever. Thank you, and good luck this week."

Ian received a standing ovation afterward, and not a dry eye was had in the room that night. As proud as I was for Ian, I also knew it was just the beginning as we had a tough road ahead of us in keeping this going.

Ian Giving His Speech at The Rolex Junior All-American Dinner
November 18, 2018

154

An ironic twist to this story was the AJGA 2019 recipient of the Jerry Cole Sportsmanship award James Roller, from Jenks, Oklahoma, finished second to Ian when Ian won UHY LLP AJGA Junior event in Eureka, MO in 2018. I doubt the AJGA has ever had an event where this has occurred and just made his victory even more special. James eventually signed with the nation's #1 ranked men's golf program, Texas Tech, in 2020. Congratulations, James, on raising over $15,000 to benefit the College Golf Fellowship and the ACE Grant program!

Building a Legacy

Seth never took to the game of golf. We played a few times as a family, and he just never seemed to enjoy playing the game. So, for us to come up with a scholarship emphasizing Seth, yet honoring Ian's golf achievements was a bit of a challenge. Around 2018 we decided to set up The Prairie Golf Scholarship Fund through the Greater Cedar Rapids Community Foundation. The fund would be used to provide a $1,000 scholarship to a college-bound senior on the Prairie boys golf team. Unlike other scholarships, ours was not tied solely to academic success, as so many are.

As of 2018, The Greater Cedar Rapids Community Foundation had approximately $173 million in assets and had provided 1,594 total grants amounting to over $11 million dollars during that year. Not wanting at that time to set up our own 501(c)(3), this made great sense.

We were looking to identify and reward an individual that embodied community activity, a passion for helping others, and an overall positive influence among their peers. The plan was to surprise Coach Erik Columbus at the upcoming Golf Banquet in October 2018. We had identified an individual on the team to be our first recipient, of which we were calling The Ian Johnston & Seth Carnicle Golf

Scholarship Fund. Senior Jared Tjelmeland was the first recipient and a great representative of what we were trying to instill in these young men. I am honored Coach Columbus has allowed me the ability to present this scholarship each year at the year-end banquet. As of this book-writing, it was announced the 2019 winners were senior twin brothers Alec and Collin Brockmeyer. Congrats to the Brockmeyer twins and best of luck continuing your academic and golf careers at Coe College in Cedar Rapids, Iowa.

Coach Erik Columbus, Jared Tjelmeland, and Ian at the 2018 Prairie Golf Award Banquet.

Both Ian and Jared had qualified as individuals in 2018 to play in the State Championship. The team missed qualifying by a few shots, but Ian and Jared were fortunate enough to go. It was the first time in school history two players had qualified as individuals to play at State. The two seniors had a very memorable experience even though day two got rained out at the 2018 Iowa State Tournament at Brown Deer Golf Course in Coralville, Iowa.

At the banquet the next week, we were very excited to present the scholarship to Coach Columbus and announce the winner. Jared was very pleased and surprised to win this award, and it was a special moment for us to present this to his family. However, unbeknownst to us, we were the ones in for a surprise!

After we announced the scholarship, we were told that the coaches had a special surprise for us. Coach Columbus and Coach Mitch Lorenz (a past Prairie golfer) proudly acknowledged the addition of the *Ian Johnston Award* to be added to the awards given each year during the banquet. The award would be presented "for excellence in the classroom, the community, and on the course." Isaac Rubsam was the first recipient of the *Ian Johnston Award.*

I stand in awe of the incredible, positive momentum this whole tragedy has provided us. The goodwill and altruism have been life-altering and so inspiring. It is further proof that out of chaos, great things are often born. Thank you,

Coaches Columbus and Lorenz, for naming such an award after Ian and thank you for the tremendous memories we had with Ian representing the Prairie Hawks in the best manner he could.

Ian with the Ian Johnston Award

I am not sure Ian fully understands the magnitude and significance of actually having an award named after you before you've even graduated high school and not posthumously for that matter. An unbelievable acknowledgment that comes with the responsibility of continuing to do good from now on as well. I said to Ian and Roman, "This is evidence that no matter what happens to you, there is always a way to do good. To stay positive and value the opportunities presented to us each day, at this moment."

Later Ian's senior year, we were notified he was a finalist for Iowa Player of the Year in 4A Boys golf. The top three players nominated were Mathew Garside (University of Iowa) of Bettendorf and Nick Pittman (Drake) from Johnston. Both of these junior golfers had become good friends of Ian's; it was an honor to be included in that evening's events. The banquet in Des Moines was a night to remember as it was hosted by Cedar Rapid's own and Hall of Fame NFL quarterback Kurt Warner. Although Ian did not win (congrats Matt!), it was nice to end a tremendous senior year for him as he became Prairie's first-ever Boy's 1st Team All-State golfer, set the school stroke average for a season at 36.6 and led the State of Iowa with an 18 hole average of 71. For a career, he was a four-time MVP and holds the 9-hole school record at 33 and the 1st, 2nd, 3rd, and 6th place school stroke average records. Seth would have been so very proud of his little brother, all 6' 5" of him!

A final honor of his high school career was bestowed upon Ian at the Prairie Senior Awards Ceremony was being selected as Prairie's 2019 recipient of the prestigious *The Bernie Saggau Award*. "Presented annually to the graduating student who best exemplifies a patriotic spirit, with strong religious and moral convictions, living and professing the qualities of honesty, integrity, and sportsmanship, believing that both games and life should be conducted by the rules."

I recently received an email from The Association of Fundraising Professionals (AEF) Eastern Iowa Chapter and was informed of some very exciting news. The National Philanthropy Day Selection Committee had selected Ian as the 2020 Outstanding Philanthropic Youth Award recipient! I continue to be amazed how all this has played out since that dreary day back in 2016. National Philanthropy day is a special day set aside each fifteenth of November. The purpose of this day is to recognize the great contributions of philanthropy "to the enrichment of the world." In digging a bit deeper I realized Zach and Kim Johnson won the Outstanding Individual Philanthropist award in 2008. Very ironic and humbling that in the same year Zach Johnson is awarded the 2020 Payne Stewart award Ian is named 2020 Outstanding Philanthropic Youth recipient! More proof that one passion, golf in this case, can open the doors of opportunity to do some great stuff in the face of adversity. I had no idea that the original GoFundMe Me, established just five days after Seth's death, would blossom into the rewarding and impactful odyssey we all have embarked on. I can only imagine what the future has in store for us!

We were starting to pursue creative ways to raise awareness and funds to continue this cause. My brother, Dan, is what I would call a modern-day Crocodile Dundee. For those unaware or too young to know who this was, Crocodile Dundee was a fictional character played by Paul Hogan in a 1986 movie titled by that same name. He was basically a man of the outdoors and could pretty much do it all, and I always compared brother Dan to this character. Dan can hit a mouse in the dark by spitting a nail through a straw and, at the same time, fight off a bear with dental floss. Maybe a bit of an exaggeration, but I am not far off.

Nonetheless, Dan, using his outdoor prowess, came up with a great idea to offer a fly-fishing class raising money for our scholarship and ASAC. Dan has given fly-fishing courses all over the country to high flying corporate execs and to your regular small-town fisherman groups. The event was held on a windy and cold day in April 2019 with good attendance for a first-time event. I believe we raised over four thousand dollars that afternoon. Thank you, Dan and St. Croix, for helping with this event!

Dan Instructing The Fly Fishing Class

Part of the group at the fly fishing event

Next up was a golf tournament. August 10th, 2019, we had our First Annual Johnston Carnicle Golf Fundraiser at, of course, Airport National Golf Course in Cedar Rapids. Again, we raised another $6,600, which was eventually equally donated to ASAC and our Scholarship Fund. We had a full field, and many local businesses stepped up to donate time and money, which we were very fortunate to have community involvement. Molly Nordlocken and Linda

Elliff, two of our key stakeholders at our company, Premier Investments, were instrumental in helping run and organize the event. Thanks, Molly and Linda!

Johnston Carnicle Golf Fundraiser
Airport National Public Golf Course
Saturday August 10th, 2019

During this time, I was looking at ways to keep holding these events yet have more structure in regard to future events and even speaking engagements. I could see a need to eventually have my own non-profit 501(c)(3) organization. I thought and pondered different names and ideas and settled on what I thought encompasses what we are ultimately trying to accomplish. That is "a network of passion-driven individuals and organizations to promote and encourage healthy lifestyle choices for young adults and education for parents through sharing our inspiring

story." Thus, Choices Network, Ltd. was born. 100% of any profits from this book will be donated to Choices Network, Ltd. to continue assisting us in raising awareness for substance abuse and addiction issues so prevalent today. We are to consist of 5 board members, but we are adding a unique, non-voting position to the organization. This will be called our Youth Ambassador.

The Youth Ambassador will be a high school student with the hope this person will help us bridge the communication of addiction and substance abuse from teenagers to parents. I believe getting a younger person's perspective will help us see what being on the front lines is really about. Most of us, as parents, are clueless and naive about what is going on in the hallways at our children's high schools. I know I was with Seth. For our first-ever Youth Ambassador, I didn't have to go very far to find. Seth's little brother, Roman, was a natural choice and took no convincing on my part to ask for his involvement.

Roman as Youth Ambassador for Choices Network, Ltd.

Roman is doing his part to continue raising awareness and promote Choices Network, Ltd. by coming up with an idea for a benefit concert. His plan involves an outdoor concert with some of his friends that share a passion and love for music. He hopes to make this an annual event. The simple fact he and Ian are doing so much when the choice wouldn't have been so favorable is awe-inspiring to me. Young people with passions can do amazing things!

My initial plan is to use our organization to travel and speak to as many different groups as we can handle. I want to have topics geared towards younger audiences all the way to parents and pretty much any group that will hear our story. As I write this book, I am working on developing a program to help guide adolescents and parents through the decision-making process when confronted with difficult choices.

Sometimes we awaken from an intense dream with our brains spinning in a frenzy of attention and awareness. Brain neurons firing on all cylinders. OK, this may be just me, but hear me out. Often that dream or idea fades away as the coffee flows and the anticipation of the day heats up. Rarely have I ever woken up, grabbed a pen and paper, and started writing, but on an early July morning in 2020, I did just that. I was holed up in a hotel room in Ames, Iowa, getting ready to watch Ian play in a golf tournament the next day. His tee time was 11:40 am, but for some reason, I woke up, intently focused at 5:22 am. I was so surprised I even wrote the exact time down on the notebook I had by the bed. It was that moment the **Don't Start Initiative (DSI)** sprang alive in my head. The DSI was the glue that was going to hold all of this together. I needed an idea, an easily remembered process for adults and adolescents to recall when confronted with making tough choices. I can't explain how this occurred, but I clearly knew why.

What I ultimately envision is a system or process that an adolescent can use when confronted with a decision that, for adults, clearly has a right or a wrong outcome. Choices like having a beer after the football game, lying to your parents, and skipping school, smoking a joint, or vaping for the first time. These may not be decisions that at the moment, by themselves, result in your demise but are decisions that can send you down a road that has life-altering outcomes. Since the DSI involves not starting in the first place, my focus would be aimed at those prior to the age of first use - commonly believed to be age 14.

As part of the DSI, I want to develop a quick 3-step process that can easily be remembered by the acronym **ABC**. The moment a teen is confronted with a big decision, they can quickly assess the situation using the ABC process. ABC stands for:

Awareness & Acknowledgment

This is the realization that you are aware that you have been offered a choice. You have the ability to say yes or no. For example, if someone offers you a joint for the first time.

You are now aware you must make a decision. You acknowledge you have 100% control of you at all times.

Breathe

In my meditation practices, I have learned that simply breathing, in the heat of any moment, provides clarity and gives you time to process your emotions. Breathing allows you the opportunity to delay, wait, postpone an answer to any question posed to you. It does not have to be very long. While breathing, I want you to think of this. It may be graphic, and that is precisely why I think it will help. **Walk or Chalk**. In other words, put into your mind a picture of an outline on the cement in white chalk of a human body. We have all seen them. Walk or Chalk. Burn that mental image into your brain at that moment.

Choose

Make your choice. There is no middle ground. You will either choose to say no and walk away, or you will choose to say yes. Choices precede consequences.

My hope is that these kids can see, with the help of our story and Seth's plight, that the best answer is to say no. However, I have learned from being a parent that telling our kids not to do something doesn't always work very well.

It may end up being the exact reason why they started in the first place.

Instead of threatening our kids and trying to scare them with punishment, maybe we should arm them with a different way to look at these situations. Give them the tools to engage with themselves and develop mechanisms for making better choices. As I alluded earlier, it isn't about never making bad choices; it's about avoiding the ones that lead to terrible outcomes. I am hopeful - or let's say I have faith - that teaching the ABC method through the Don't Start Initiative can add another arrow in the quiver to help adolescents.

I think about choices all the time, how all of our lives are influenced and eventually dictated by the choices we make. As a popular tv personality always says, "When you choose the behavior, you choose the consequences." This is so correct. I recall so many times saying those or similar phrases to all the boys.

As I discussed earlier, nature vs. nurture is another popular psychological debate. Is this about genetic inheritance or environmental factors? Who do we blame? I don't know for sure as the only evidence I have is what happened to us when poor choices were made within our family. There are numerous examples of those who had horrendously difficult childhoods yet never succumbed to the seducing of addictions, and there are those who grew up in the iconic "Leave it to Beaver" households that fell prisoner to addiction and substance abuse.

I feel I have a duty, an obligation to Seth to try to find deeper context to all of this and to prevent this from happening to another family ultimately. This isn't all on Seth; we all have some ownership as family members. Trust me - I am aware that his death truly becomes terminal when I stop learning and searching for clarity, not just for others but for myself.

The Struggle Within

"If people are good only because they fear punishment,
and hope for a reward, then we are a sorry lot indeed."
- Albert Einstein

It is my thirty-first year in the financial advisory field, and I
genuinely love what I do. I run a wealth management firm
beautifully situated in the middle of flyover America, Cedar
Rapids, Iowa. I started the company, Premier Investments
of Iowa, Inc., fresh out of college at the age of 23. My best
friend, Brock Renner, joined me about 25 years ago, and
we have never looked back. With no money and no clients,
we now employ six full-time employees and have nine
financial advisors. The people I have been fortunate to
meet, to work with, and to build something from nothing
are numerous, and I am very grateful to have been part of
this with them.

However, this book isn't about running a successful small
business or how to make more money; there are plenty of
those. I am not sure all the business success and fame in
the world will make you happy, profoundly happy.
**Especially if you have unattended issues with substance
abuse and addiction.** Often that same financial success
will support those issues left neglected, as is the case with

many well-known famous actors, athletes, and professionals.

Iconic rock legend, Kurt Cobain, and lead singer from the '90s grunge band, Nirvana, committed suicide at the young age of 27. From the outside, he appeared to be on top of the world. In his suicide note, he stressed loneliness, unhappiness, and guilt. He had alcohol and drug addiction issues for years and had been in and out of rehab. Unfortunately, the road to financial success and fame is paved with many a lost soul.

"For example, when we're backstage, and the lights go out, and the manic roar of the crowds begins... The fact is, I can't fool you, or any of you, it simply isn't fair to you or me... I need to be slightly numb in order to regain the enthusiasm I once had as a child... I don't have the passion anymore, and so remember, it's better to burn out than to fade away."
- excerpts from Kurt Cobain's suicide note

More recently, on June 8th, 2018, celebrity chef Anthony Bourdain committed suicide by hanging himself while filming an episode for his award-winning "Parts Unknown" television series while in Kaysersberg, France. He had battled substance abuse and addiction issues for most of his adult life. His mother, Gladys Bourdain, was quoted in an interview with The New York Times as saying, "he is absolutely the last person in the world I would have ever dreamed would do something like this." She echoes the same sentiment I had when discussing Sam Gerry's courageous personal admissions of depression and suicidal ideation earlier. It's occasionally the ones we least suspect that end up having the most destructive thoughts. We all play a crucial role in identifying and reaching out to help those in need before it becomes too late.

Don't be lured into the illusion of what money or success may bring. This book is really about you and embracing the opportunity in front of you to create more meaning and fulfillment in your life. It's about learning and letting go at the same time; and about being human, having passion, and about love.

I read books obsessively; in some ways, it has become a positive addiction for me. I read mostly non-fiction books ranging from Sam Harris' New York Times Bestseller, "Waking Up" to "The Behavioral Investor" by Daniel Crosby, PhD. I like to read books on a variety of topics and from a variety of perspectives, so I don't fall into the confirmation bias trap so prevalent in today's society. Part of my learning process throughout this timeline has been challenging myself to learn and adopt new methods of becoming self-aware. It has led me to some very beneficial coping mechanisms, like meditation, which I will discuss later on.

As a financial advisor for over three decades, I have had the opportunity to meet some very "successful" people. The perfect retirement scenario is a delicate balance between mastering the financial and the emotional aspects of the transition from work to relaxation. It's undesirable to have only one or the other. Far too often, I see people with plenty of financial resources, yet they are unfulfilled with their lives. They are never happy with their relationship with money. I call these people financial hoarders.

You know them. These are the people who have reached a personal summit in adding to their hoard of money, yet they are addicted to watching it grow, yes, **addicted**. Afraid to derive any type of pleasure with their money, feeling guilty to enjoy life. Not much different than a compulsive gambler who is never satisfied with their winnings. It's never enough. The financial hoarder and the compulsive gambler both have similar addiction traits it would seem. Getting people you care about to make positive changes is often very challenging, especially influencing behavior the older we get. "You can't teach an old dog new tricks," it is often said.

This aspect of human behavior has been studied by psychologists and is often quoted by economists, commonly referred to as the sunk cost fallacy. This is the concept that your decisions are blinded by the emotional investments you accumulate, and the more you have invested in something, the more difficult it becomes to let go of it. The misconception is that we make rational decisions based on the future value of investments, and experiences. I see this concept permeate over into my financial advisory practice.

People hold onto poor investments too long or sell good investments too early. Greed and fear are not good investment strategies, and I can't imagine they are good foundations for personal decision making in other aspects of life. I am from the school of thought of using more inspirational methods, some of which deserve more exploration from me in the future.

Behavioral finance is a fast-evolving area in the financial planning industry. A great book I recently finished, one I highly recommend, is Daniel Crosby's "The Behavioral Investor." One of the best books on the topic I have ever read. The "why" behind money decisions has always been of great interest to me. In speaking with investment clients over the years, I often discuss ways to change or influence human behavior. I believe there are two main ways to influence human behavior. You can **inspire,** or you can **scare** people into a belief or into changing a belief. The financial markets do this daily by the endless and often unnecessary, second-by-second reporting of the stock market. What should be a long term (20+ years) proposition is announced like a 2-minute horse race. It's insane and a complete waste of time for the average investor. Greed (inspire) and fear (scare) are thrown at us all day long, and it's not just the financial media. This goes hand in hand with our fast-paced, overstimulated, addicted society.

In January 2018 I was approached by InvestmentNews magazine to discuss the impact within the financial advisory industry of the opioid epidemic. In a story by Greg Iacurci titled, "Advisers struck by the opioid crisis seek to get the word out to peers and their communities" I discussed, along with other advisors impacted by this issue, what we have noticed and how we can promote positive change. As Mr. Iacurci alluded to in his story, "A recent InvestmentNews investigation uncovered how financial advisers are increasingly being drawn into the crisis. Not only can addiction wreak havoc on a clients' finances, sometimes to the tune of hundreds of thousands of dollars, but advisers are uniquely positioned to spot signs of financial exploitation and erratic or unusual behavior from clients that can be traced to the opioid epidemic." I later added, "I can teach people how to invest money, but if I can get people to change their behavior towards addiction, that's my true calling." With that in mind I reached out to Daniel Crosby, PhD to see if he'd be willing to discuss how addictions and relationships with money go hand in hand. He graciously accepted my invitation to discuss these matters. Dr. Crosby is a highly respected and a leading authority in the behavioral finance world, it also didn't hurt that I have been a huge fan of his books over the years.

I was particularly interested in how he viewed addiction (to money) within the context of the disease and choice models, as well as ways, if any, we can influence behavior to result in healthier and more productive overall outcomes. We discussed my concept of the "financial hoarder" and the compulsive gambler and if he thought there were similarities and commonalities between the two. I thought it was interesting he mentioned, "a lot of why we approach addictions from a disease model is because we don't stigmatize disease." In the Addiction chapter I discussed how harmful putting labels on people can be and now this was resurfacing with the observation Dr. Crosby put forth. Does labeling addiction as a disease allow those afflicted to take less personal responsibility for their behavior? We both agreed that the environment plays a large role, yet he so aptly added that, "disease often takes behavioral activation as well. Everything in psychology is a combination of biology and environment." Along with the genetic/environment component, choices still and always do exist.

This was exactly what I was looking for and was the reason I felt it necessary to talk with him. Later in our conversations he discussed the fact that there is a physiological component in narcotics that isn't present in money. So, is the compulsive gambler an addict by the disease model or is gambling just addictive and more of a choice? Obviously how you define "addiction" and "disease" will guide you in the direction of an answer. Unfortunately, this isn't the book for me to really expand and dive into this in the manner I wish. Dr. Crosby left me with a number of good books to read and suggested I look into The Perma Model approach to happiness designed by American psychologist and educator Martin Seligman. Positive Psychology, the scientific study of the "good life", or the positive aspects of the human experience is another discipline suggested from him for me to pursue.

I wish to express my sincere appreciation to Daniel Crosby, PhD for allowing me the time to tap into his wealth of insight on these very intriguing issues and concerns.

Addictions can encompass many aspects of life. They aren't monopolized by just alcohol and drugs. I know this because, in my late 20s and early 30s, I was an addict, not to drugs or alcohol, but I became something equally unacceptable and devastating, a compulsive gambler. I understand that in my profession, this is not something you put on a resume; however, at this stage of my life and career, I really don't mind discussing. It was part of my past, yet also part of my story today.

I am fallible, but more importantly, I confessed to **MYSELF** I had a problem, and I addressed it. I won't go into any detail other than admitting to you now that I knew I had a problem, and I made the necessary adjustments in my life, and I never looked back. I believe poor choices can only be cemented as mistakes if I don't learn and grow from them. I never tried drugs or smoked pot. It wasn't because I knew I wouldn't like them; it was because I was smart enough to know I would. I didn't want to become multi-addicted in a sense as I firmly believed with ADD, I had the potential to get in trouble with this. See, I told you I was going, to be honest with you. We all fight something, and if you don't realize what it is yet, then I suggest you go have a very intense, honest conversation with the person in the mirror, someone you cannot lie to.

Being honest with yourself by admitting you have substance abuse or addiction issues is the first step to recovery. We require those we know to be honest with us, yet at our inner core, we often aren't honest with ourselves. A 2019 article in Forbes magazine by Paloma Cantero-Gomez highlights the top ten traits we most admire in others:

1. Humility
2. Ability to learn
3. **Integrity (Honesty)**
4. Responsibility
5. Resiliency
6. Compassion for others
7. Respect for others
8. Big vision
9. Inspiring others
10. Reinventing yourself

As you can see, being honest ranks very high on admirable traits in relationships. Yet, when someone's honesty towards you impinges on your bad habits, well, then that's somehow unwarranted, and we tend to get defensive. We really can't have it both ways, can we? It's often hard to be honest with those who struggle with addiction and substance abuse issues without sounding judgmental or condescending; it is a delicate dance for sure.

Often when you feel as if your life is going to plan and you are on target to accomplish your hopes and dreams, some event happens. It's called life. It happens to all of us eventually, and it comes in many forms, such as getting fired, divorced, injured, or even worse death. On January 26, 2020, we lost nine beautiful souls in a helicopter crash in the hills outside Calabasas, California, on a foggy early morning. Beloved basketball star Kobe Bryant, age 41, and his daughter Gianna Bryant, age 13, were among those on the helicopter when it crashed. I was a few months into writing this book, and this event had a profound impact on me, motivating me to finish writing.

It reinforced my belief that our time on this beautiful sphere, adrift in the vast unknown, is very, very short. On Valentine's Day 1990, the Voyager 1 spacecraft looked back to earth after flying by Jupiter and Saturn on its way out of the solar system and took one of the most awe-inspiring photos ever. It is still the most distant picture ever taken of Earth. Seeing "the pale blue dot" photograph as it's called, humbly reminds us of the fragility of human existence and the fact we are all in this together. Looking at this photo makes me wonder if that pale blue dot somehow disappeared, would the universe even notice or actually miss us? Are we really that important? I still like to believe so!

"Pale Blue Dot" image taken by the Voyager 1
Image credit: NASA/JPL-Caltech

I embraced my freedom from alcohol on Dec 24th, 2017. I don't necessarily look at it as giving up alcohol, as that would insinuate something being sacrificed. Giving up alcohol is no sacrifice; in fact, for me, it's a gift. I wouldn't say it's been super easy as the absence of having a glass of wine and a cigar while grilling on those hot, Iowa summer evenings is something I do occasionally miss. Having a cat named Opus (after my favorite cabernet) and a dog named Caymus (my second favorite cabernet) has made this slightly more exacting. Now, it's still the cigar, just a different beverage of choice.

According to the National Institute on Alcohol Abuse and Alcoholism, the daily guideline for men is no more than four drinks in a day and no more than fourteen drinks in a week. Well, I guess by that definition, I was an alcoholic and had been for many years. This may sound like an old adage, but I don't go to meetings, and I don't really feel the urge to drink. I have attended AA meetings in support of others who need my attention, yet I have personally found enough reasons and motivations for me to quit. I may start drinking again in the future, or I may never have a drink again. I don't have a long-term goal. I just know for this point in my life I won't support that industry in any way. I know in this regard I am probably an anomaly as I was able to quit cold turkey. As I look back, I can clearly see how my life has become substantially better without alcohol in it. Ironically, it was brought to my attention the title of this book, "This One's for You," is something you'd say while hoisting a beverage in honor of someone as a toast. Indeed, it is, just non-alcoholic for me!

I did have an incident in my past that I am not proud of that involved alcohol. Over 20 years ago, I had an OWI charge that has since disappeared from my record. In my early 30s, I was on the way home after a birthday party late one night, and I was pulled over by the police. I refused the breathalyzer test (I'm sure I was over the limit), and at that time, the laws assumed guilt if you refuse the test. Enduring a very frightening night in jail, I plead guilty and subsequently lost my license for nine months. After expensive fees and court costs, I resumed driving and had a breathalyzer installed in my car for a year. I ultimately took a required alcohol education class, which was coincidentally held at ASAC, and ended up doing community service at a public library. It was a pretty low time in my life, during which I learned that poor choices do have consequences. I don't recommend it, but spending a night in jail can quickly bring even the most fearless and confident person back to reality. Definitely not one of my proudest moments, but for sure, one of the most impactful.

One learning aspect of this whole journey is the stark reality that I needed to focus on myself first, or I would have a tough time making it through all of this. I would be of little help to those that needed my attention the most if I didn't take care of myself. That is one of the reasons I was drawn to meditation, as I will discuss later.

I often think of the scenario on an airplane when the airline attendant explains, "in the event of an air pressure change, an oxygen mask will drop down from the compartment above you. Secure your mask first, before assisting anyone with you." What they are trying to say is that you are of little help to your loved ones if you aren't around to help. My health has become my top concern, and I have invested a tremendous amount of time and energy in that regard since Seth's death. At fifty-four, I physically feel better and am emotionally stronger than I have been in years. I thank Seth for giving me the inspiration.

The Evolution of Self

I'd be remiss if I didn't take a short detour in discussing some very personal internal dialog and challenges I have encountered while on this journey. I may jump around a bit, but that's just my ADD kicking in; don't worry, it's harmless. My road to trying to understand all this, especially Seth's addiction and eventual death, was very inconsistent and volatile at a minimum. As time passed, I learned to develop ways to compartmentalize my feelings and, along the way, discovered it was ok to allow myself to get lost in grief. The key was keeping the **length of time I grieved very short.** In other words, expressing intense sorrow, anger, and deep pain is fine and healthy, I allowed myself to feel those emotions, I just wasn't allowing it to linger very long or define who I was becoming, in a negative way. The pain of Seth's death was unavoidable, but the duration of the suffering, in my opinion, was mostly optional.

A guiding influence in writing this book was to use **MY** experiences, good and bad, to see if I could help make a difference in the way families deal with substance abuse and addictions, specifically the suffering that goes along with this disease. Substance abuse and addictions don't discriminate, judge, or have any religious affiliations. The struggle for me, like many others, hasn't been in identifying the problem, it's been more in trying to find some solutions.

We are all a phone call or doctor visit away from the stark reminder of our mortality. I cannot stress enough the importance of developing coping skills with trauma and death **before the event actually happens**. It's such a proactive discipline to learn and practice as opposed to being woefully unprepared to deal with life's stresses and surprises when they inevitably happen. It goes back to having a positive mindset and a realistic view of life and death. Fortunately, it is possible to achieve this state of mind regardless of your unique and personal convictions.

I have always been more inclined to seek out the answer's to life's big questions for myself rather than be told what to think. I may be a bit stubborn and slightly headstrong, yet to be honest, it has been a blessing for me. I often find myself asking *why* and *how* and continuously pushing myself to keep learning, relentlessly seeking ways to improve my life and understanding my meaning and purpose. Being content is not in my DNA, and I have often been accused of not being able to sit still for very long, mostly by my lovely mom, Gerry. I am quite certain, in this regard, I am not alone. I am sure many of you catch yourself questioning closely held personal beliefs and, in the past, had the courage to challenge authority at certain times during your life. It's normal to do so and makes humans a very adaptable and emerging species.

Spirituality means many things to many people. Broadly defined, it represents a sense of connection to something bigger than ourselves, typically a **personal** search for meaning in life. I am currently on a quest to discover my own meaning and how I can positively assist others in finding theirs. I doubt I have discovered anything earth-shattering, yet I have committed to approaching this with an open mind and will never stop searching, always learning.

In my research for "This One's For You," I have encountered amazing individuals, seen some incredible human achievements, and witnessed a few extremely passionate people surviving tremendous personal setbacks with the utmost courage. I stand in awe of these people, and I am curiously attempting to understand why some people have figured this out, and others haven't.

I have often been approached to attend Alcoholics Anonymous meetings in the past. I have always been intrigued and impressed by the vulnerability of the individuals I have met at these meetings. The sheer honesty that is expressed is quite humbling, and if you have not attended such a meeting, I strongly suggest you find the time to do so. I am impressed with the way they approach the concept of a "higher power" and the willingness for A.A. to help all those afflicted regardless of religious doctrine.

There are so many uniquely personal factors that seem to go into what someone believes in. Personal experiences, place of birth, family history, and educational differences help form what we all eventually will believe. Often, a "higher power" can be interpreted as looking from within as well.

The original Big Book, known as "**Alcoholics Anonymous: The story of how over 100 men have recovered from alcoholism,**" was released in 1939 and has sold over 20 million copies. I applaud A.A. in understanding not all alcoholics and addicts are the same, and they are often uniquely dissimilar in their spirituality and religious beliefs, rightfully so. As I alluded to earlier, the grim reality is that the monster grip of substance abuse, addictions and alcoholism does not differentiate and couldn't care less about what you believe. To attempt to win this fight, we need to attack this from ALL possible angles and perspectives, which begins in discovering and committing

to your own personal convictions and faith yet
simultaneously respecting those of other opinions. Once
you've discovered your motivations and have impassioned
your heart and mind, you will be capable of herculean,
unstoppable personal growth, pulling up those around you
at the same time. It can be quite extraordinary and life-
altering!

For me, it was the moment I became aware that I did not
have all the answers to personal enlightenment, and I
certainly wasn't smart enough to claim I did. As an ancient
Chinese Philosopher, Lao Tzu, so humbly conceded, "to
realize that you do not understand is a virtue; not to realize
that you do not understand is a defect." I firmly assert and
submit to you that it is extremely difficult, if not
impossible, to advance as a society when we have
competing groups holding non-negotiable beliefs that
are mutually exclusive. It's a witch's cauldron of
malevolence, disdain, contempt, spite, malice, and doubt. It
provides nothing solid to build a strong societal foundation
on; if anything, it's eroding us slowly from the inside.

There are so many different scenarios and alternatives
provided, yet at the end of the day we really, truly don't
know what happens when we die, or at least I don't. The
only two certainties for me are that those left behind will

mourn and will struggle to make sense of my death and what meaning I find in my life while I am alive is up solely up to me.

There is little doubt that our personal views and thoughts on dying will influence and frame the actions of our lives in the present. The shadow of death casts back on our lives as a blunt reminder of what awaits us all. This perspective ought to give us pause and awareness of the true fragility of our beings and even possibly our species. The good news is your inclination in what you believe will happen when you are gone shouldn't prohibit you from forming good habits and leading a very inspired life. Let me provide an example of what I am trying to say.

If you are living your life with divine inspiration and a vivid understanding of what awaits you in the afterlife, a clear mission as to why you are here, then I assume you are trying your best to make sure that this is the place you will eventually end up? Heaven, in this regard, is the final destination on your celestial journey. It would make sense that you would live an inspired life in the here and now. The motivation and desire to do good and to lead others by example ought to come into sharp focus if the odyssey through eternity is known to you.

However, if you are reluctant to subscribe to any form of an afterlife, as some do, you should have tremendous appreciation and gratitude for what you have now, as this is the only life you will ever have. With that perspective, I imagine you are inclined to look at life, now, as a true gift not to be wasted. I submit to you that either personally held belief system, right or wrong, has the potential to allow the individual to live a very inspired life and to do good.

Author and the Zen Hospice Project co-founder Frank Ostaseski writes about this in his best-selling book The Five Invitations: Discovering what death can teach us about living fully. Drawing on the tenants of Buddhism, he considers the inseparability of life and death:

> "We cannot be truly alive without maintaining an awareness of death. Death is not waiting for us at the end of a long road. Death is always with us, in the marrow of every passing moment. She is the secret teacher hiding in plain sight. She helps us to discover what matters most."

Drawing on personal healing and work with the dying, Ostaseski outlines his five "invitations" through which an acceptance of death opens a healthier relationship with life:

1. Don't wait
2. Welcome everything, push away nothing
3. Bring your whole self to the experience
4. Find a place of rest in the middle of things
5. Cultivate "don't-know" mind

A good book to help assist those looking for additional guidance and understanding of death. There certainly can't be too many options for those in need of solace and peace. As I have alluded to throughout this book, preparing and respecting the inevitability of suffering (death) is, I believe, a key to how you will ultimately handle it when it occurs to those important to you.

Why does all this matter? How does this relate to what we went through in the death of a child? Let me conclude this discussion with faith. **We all have faith.** Faith, a French word, is "the trust in something or a strong belief system." Faith, for many, has a religious or more spiritual connotation and is an awesome supplier of human desire, motivation, and inspiration. I wish we had more of it in many of us today. Faith can also evoke a different sentiment as well. For example, I had faith that Adderall, when prescribed to Seth, would help with his ADD, and becoming addicted wouldn't be an issue. Ian had faith he would make that putt to secure the State Tournament in

2017, and for that matter, my dad has faith the Chicago Cubs will win the World Series (every year), and The Iowa Hawkeyes will win the National Championship (all sports I may add). Blind faith or something else would be attributed to him :)

We need to be careful as faith can occasionally blind us to reality. We often see and interpret what we want to see. It seems apparent to me that, as we gain knowledge on a topic and eventually form an emotional belief system, we then seek out ways to try to validate this belief. Confirmation bias is a common practice for most of us. We enjoy watching and reading about ideas and concepts we already have developed and formed. It's not an abnormality in any way, it's more a function of how we, as humans, are innately wired. It's less stressful and more rewarding to watch, listen, and read things that validate or reinforce our current belief system. For this, we are all guilty. However, we didn't progress to where we are as a society today by locking the doors to our minds!

A very good friend of mine and fellow board member of Choices Network, Ltd., Kenyon Murray, so aptly phrased faith as "the substance of things hoped for and the evidence of things not seen." It's no surprise the word faith itself is rife with ambiguity and subjectivity. Faith is a very personal notion, one that each of us, rightfully so, shouldn't relinquish easily. Since Seth's death, I have been forced to consider new beliefs and challenge previously held ones. All in all, I feel like I have achieved tremendous growth in these areas, and I am very excited to continue learning. As for now, I am at peace (but not content!) with my spirituality, and **I have the utmost faith I am honoring Seth the best way I can**.

I am confident that the urge to seek answers increases as we age. According to the Successful AGing Evaluation study (SAGE) that was conducted from Jan 2013-June 2014, "Finding meaning in one's life constitutes a sound strategy for thriving in later years - in part because it supports the preservation of a person's physical and mental well-being." In other words, humans will always be curious; I guess that's what makes us human.

I mentioned earlier I have been gifted with a positive attitude my whole life and an unwavering level of confidence in my fellow man. For that, I am fortunate. However, at the same time, I have been accused of being unrealistic (always glass half full), and for that, I am working on being more attentive and becoming a better listener.

Maybe there is some validity to this. I stumbled across a very interesting article about the concept of toxic positivity. Is it actually possible to be too positive? Alarmingly, based on some medical professionals and therapists, this concept is not only alive but probably has renewed interest due to the worldwide Covid-19 pandemic. Toxic positivity is the idea that you should spend your focus only on positive emotions and only the most positive aspects of your life. The detractors of this concept believe this thought process oversimplifies how the human brain processes emotions and can actually be detrimental to our mental health. Great, now I am too positive? I guess if you look hard enough, you'll find information that always presents another side of any belief. At this point I will stick to being too positive and overly optimistic, I know of no other way!

I have, as far as I can remember, believed in the power of self-overcoming, yet the past eight years pushed me to be willing to pursue many different ideologies and beliefs. As I hinted in a previous chapter, for me, death seemed to open the floodgates of inquiry and investigation even further.

"I do not fear death. I had been dead for billions and billions of years before I was born, and had not suffered the slightest inconvenience from it."
- Mark Twain

I tell Roman and Ian this all the time - mentally prepare yourself to be strong enough to learn from pain and suffering; it's right around the corner. When it happens to you as a child or teenager, it can become your competitive advantage over those who haven't had the opportunity to embrace it, be fearless.

"I judge you unfortunate because you have never lived through misfortune. You have passed through life without an opponent-no one can ever know what you are capable of, not even you."
- Seneca

I appreciate the opportunity to expound slightly in more detail, a few of the thoughts bouncing around in my head. I still have a lot to learn, and I feel compelled to continue breaking down self-imposed barriers attempting to discover my true calling in life. I have a long way to go, but I shall remain **undeterred.**

Meditation

I began meditation in June of 2019, simply as a way to broaden my experiences and to continue my quest and thirst for knowledge. The essence of meditation is awareness and being aware creates knowledge. As I was searching for additional ways to deal with stress and anxiety, I stumbled upon meditation as a way to become more relaxed and more in tune with my surroundings, both external and internal. I use a daily meditation app that I downloaded on my phone, and each morning I commit the 10 minutes or so of uninterrupted attention. I haven't missed a day since I began.

This routine has helped me immensely, and I would strongly encourage the practice. I want to stress that I am far from an expert in this area and am learning as I go. While rare, there is a potential for negative meditation experiences. It is important that you consult with a professional instructor for anything of value or depth specific to you.

I practice what is called Mindfulness Meditation. The goal of this technique is to achieve a state of alert and focused observation by paying attention to thoughts and sensations without judgment. It involves breathing methods in combination with guided imagery to help reduce anxiety and stress. Mindfulness meditation has really taken off, and it is believed that over ten million Americans practice daily. It provides me with a sense of tranquility and has definitely helped me handle the day-to-day stressful situations with a heightened sense of confidence. I am substantially more patient with people, and I have taken time more often to simply smile and appreciate the great life I have been fortunate to experience. I have developed a very deep trust-not in something otherworldly or outside of me but in a calm sense of reality inside of me, a personal peace. It's difficult to put into words, but I have to assume many of you who are reading this know what I mean.

One great aspect of meditation is it can be whatever you want it to be. If you are religious, your belief system can be incorporated into your daily practice and discovery. I personally like the fact that I can control the narrative up to a certain extent. There is also a widespread belief that meditation can help prevent several physiological disorders, including Alzheimer's and ADD. In hindsight, I wonder if this would have been a better initial treatment for Seth other than being prescribed Adderall for his ADD? As a past board member of the Cedar Rapids Alzheimer's Association, I am very interested in acquiring additional research on this approach along with the benefits for ADD. I am also going to explore the data and information on potential implications for those in addiction and substance abuse therapy as well.

Meditation has become much more mainstream, with many popular actors and actresses, along with athletes enjoying the benefits of this discipline. Again, just because many use this practice doesn't mean it will work for you. It isn't magic or a secret weapon to achieve superhuman abilities. It's an additional arrow in your quiver to deal with stress and anxiety. I went into meditation without a specific goal in mind. In that manner, I am without judgment or trying to keep score. I have learned from meditation when we fight against the natural flow of things coming and going, we suffer needlessly. Each morning is a brand new opportunity to explore the benefits of what meditation has to offer. As they say, "I wake up an optimist."

I have spoken with many people who started out meditating with reckless enthusiasm, falsely believing they would see images or immediately transcend to a higher level. They soon get burned out and end up stopping. The issue is they had unrealistic expectations that couldn't have been met in the short amount of time they allowed this practice to incorporate into their daily lives. I am only at the beginning of my journey, and I don't think I have even come close to unlocking meditation's full potential. Although I had no specific expectations, so it would be difficult to get frustrated or become impatient.

With the incredible technological advancements and the speed of which information flows these days, it's no surprise that we are a nation of overconnected, over-stimulated individuals. We have developed very little patience, and we want results yesterday, not just today. I am convinced that the ability to know more on a topic doesn't always equate to better results. Look at diets and how much we know about what healthy foods to eat.

Never in the history of humanity have we known more about what not to eat and what to stay away from. Yet, I would argue that this information isn't helping us as a nation. Obesity and heart disease continue to be an increasing problem despite advancements in our knowledge of prevention. According to the CDC, more than one-third of adults (42.4 percent) and one-sixth (18.5 percent) of children and adolescents in the United States were affected by obesity. Why are the numbers increasing if we have so much more information? I think we know why. It's not the information, it's what we do (or don't do) with the information. Diets, fads, quick fixes do not work long term. We need a way to disconnect from information overload, step back, and look inwards.

Meditation has a way of bringing us back to the moment, to reconnect with the lost art of introspection. Think of the last time you traveled in your car, family in tow off for a vacation. How often did you look back at your children and smile as they delightfully gazed out the window as the car zipped down the highway? Eyes wide open, their young minds were deep in thought and imagination as they took the time to notice nature's beauty and the awe-inspiring scenes all around them. Yeah, right, not going to happen.

Now, back to reality. You look and see that they are paralyzed in thoughtless stimulation staring mindlessly into a device held in the palm of their sweaty hands. Faces contorted and frequently grimacing with every twitch of their fingers. Their world is a fantasy game that they are playing and living in so they don't have to think in the real world. They are seemingly oblivious to the raw allure of the artistry that surrounds them in nature. They are missing a tremendous opportunity to engage, to self-reflect, to think. We have lost this ability today, and I wonder if younger individuals are learning coping mechanisms to deal with stress and anxiety? Or are they inclined to numb their pain with drugs (includes vaping) and alcohol.

Meditation is not about being lost in thought but more the opposite as you are keenly aware of your thoughts and emotions. American author and lecturer Dan Millman says, "You don't have to control your thoughts. You just have to stop letting them control you." That is what I see meditation doing for me. We assume that we are the center of attention (and the universe) and that life moves at us fast. **The reality is life moves at the same speed. We just don't navigate slowly enough to notice and to become appreciative of what we have and who we are.** Meditation has helped me with my attention issues for which and I am intuitively more aware of my day-to-day existence. I would also add, I am much more grateful for what I have in my life.

The roots of Mindful Meditation go back thousands of years, where the teachers of Buddhism referred to the practice as "Insight Meditation." India seems to be the consensus as to where meditation originated, although many civilizations and societies profess the title. Suffice to say, meditation has had many influences and adaptations over the years and depending on what you are looking for, there is a practice or teaching suitable for most anyone.

Personally, I would like to see more children and teenagers learn the art of meditation. I know there is a push in the industry to create apps and information catered to children and adolescents. I think this is a super idea to help our youth find healthy, low-cost ways to manage stress and find a creative outlet to engage with themselves, in as little as 10 minutes a day. Better yet, they can still use their phones!

"If every 8-year-old in the world is taught meditation, we will eliminate violence from the world within one generation."
- Dalai Lama

Life Committed

There are two things I am terrified of - spiders and clowns. I have been scuba diving at one-hundred-foot depths in the ocean at night with sharks and eels, I have handled snakes, and I am not afraid of ghosts or demons. But spiders and clowns, worse yet a spider clown (apparently the internet has created such grotesque creatures). I made the mistake of telling Roman this, what I thought was a harmless fact. So, I am in my office at home working, and I notice Roman has written this motivational quote on my large whiteboard reserved for important business ideas:

I love my boys. More often than not, we need to enjoy the spontaneous humor in life! By the way Roman you spelled "lerning" wrong :)

Jim Valvano, Hall of Fame College basketball coach at North Carolina State in his powerful speech at the 1993 ESPY's, said, "To me, there are three things everyone should do every day. Number one is laugh. Number two is think - spend some time in thought. Number three, you should have your emotions move you to tears. If you laugh, think and cry, that's a heck of a day." Fifty-five days after this speech, he succumbed to cancer. His speech is regarded as one of the greatest motivational speeches of all time. We all need to pause and reflect on the depth of the human capacity those words hold today. Laugh, think, and cry. Not too much to ask, is it?

A while back, I was talking with Roman, and we were having a good, fairly deep conversation about the meaning of life. I am sure this topic has taken over many evenings discussions around the world and has probably raised more questions than answers. In our case, we were discussing morality and ethics and what are some good personal practices to live by. We somehow stumbled on the crazy notion of writing our own Ten Commandments.

Not to be in any way disparaging towards religion or the actual Ten Commandments, but just to write down some strategies or practices that would be beneficial to us and humanity, in our own words. Something that more accurately reflects the current times we live in. We refer to them as our ten principles. After some back and forth, this is what we came up with.

THE TEN PRINCIPLES
by Jeff and Roman Johnston

1. Treat your fellow humans and all living things with honesty, love, and respect. Treat children and the elderly with special tenderness, warmth, and care.
2. Be open-minded and willing to alter your beliefs with new evidence. Do not be led blindly by others. Be your own lamp.
3. Be mindful of your actions and the implications or consequences. Strive to cause no harm, unless defending oneself or absolutely necessary.
4. There is no one right way to live, but there are wrong ways: respect other's ideologies and personal beliefs.
5. Always be learning. If you are green, you grow if you are ripe, you rot. It's impossible to know everything, but it's not impossible to try.

6. Do not do unto others that of which you don't want done to you.
7. Be ALIVE, not just living. Seek enjoyment and pleasure, take the time to be in complete awe of nature.
8. Take tremendous care of your mind and body. It's the only one you got.
9. On your last breath, make sure you have left the world a better place than you found it.
10. The past is done, the future isn't won, we have today now go have fun!

Well, there you go. What an enlightening exercise! We knocked these out in a few minutes and had a lot of fun with them. I made copies and hung them up in each of the boys' bedrooms.

I often think about how fortunate I am to have my two boys, Ian and Roman. To be honest, I don't know where I would be today without them. I have unconditional sympathy for those who lose an only child. The courage to move on and find meaning is very inspiring to me. I recently read a great book by Steve Grant, "Don't forget me: A Lifeline of HOPE For Those Touched By Substance Abuse And Addiction." I highly suggest reading as it's a touching story of living a life *undeterred*. Unfathomably he lost his only two sons, Chris & Kelly, to drug overdoses. Chris died in 2005 at the age of 21. Five years later, Kelly would also succumb to this disease at the age of 24.

Mr. Grant's book was essentially reliving what our family endured multiplied by two. I could absolutely and unequivocally relate to his pain and suffering, but for two? In my eyes, he's a true hero in how he has not only survived but has done so much to raise awareness and money to help those with substance abuse and addiction issues.

Steve and I have a lot in common, and I am honored to have had an opportunity to get to know him better over the past few months. In a phone conversation recently, Steve discussed his situation and said, "the two boys died of the same thing, yet they had such different paths." Mr. Grant's foundation, Chris and Kelly's HOPE Foundation, provides financial support to programs that treat teens and young adults who struggle with substance abuse and addictions. To date, his organization has given out around **$900,00** to assist those programs working with the afflicted. **Bravo!**

He alluded to the fact that the age of first use is now 14. I immediately thought back to the young man I met that day in 2018 at the introduction of this book and recalled he was only 14 and was already a recovering alcoholic. I am honored to continue this journey with Steve Grant, and I believe, together, we can make progress and bring awareness to this issue in our society that is in great need of this type of support and education.

One of the most influential writers of his day, C.S. Lewis said, "You can't go back and change the beginning, but you can start where you are and change the ending." The fact that you can literally start over each day has to be encouraging for those who deal with anxiety and substance abuse. Each day is a new day, and all we really have is the here and now. In searching for meaning and purpose in life, I believe it's how we look at the present and how we need to learn from but let go of the past.

Just for a moment to entertain me and to have some fun as I wrap up this labor of love, go ahead and put your deep-thinking hat on. I once enjoyed these healthy discussions back in my college psychology and philosophy classes, and over time, they still resonate within me. Although I had a finance major at the University of Northern Iowa in 1989, I still fondly recall and enjoy the discussions during my philosophy classes.

Is it possible that there isn't a purpose or meaning to life? It seems inconceivable to me to be honest but certainly not impossible. Just because I can't imagine the concept or am unwilling too doesn't mean the possibility doesn't exist. Maybe, just maybe, the purpose **of life** is simply to find the meaning of our **own lives**? This idea was postulated by Viktor Frankl in "Man's Search for Meaning" many years ago, and I discussed it in one of my earlier chapters. **Your purpose and meaning in life is the only one you can control.** The rest should take care of itself.

We need answers and clarity to guide us through our daily lives, or do we? Indulge my curiosity – as we tirelessly seek answers to these questions, the mere quest to understand life and death keeps us going. Not knowing just isn't in our human DNA. Consider when in our educational lifetime, were we ever rewarded for not knowing? However, if we were to find out all the answers, where would the desire and motivation be to seek any truth, and would this new knowledge be a good thing?

In the classic 1992 film, "A Few Good Men," Jack Nicholson's character Col. Nathan R. Jessup, said, "You want answers?" Followed by Lt. Daniel Kaffee, played by Tom Cruise, "I want the truth!" Col. Jessup fired back, "You can't handle the truth!" Consider for a moment that if the truth were revealed to us and this revelation contradicted all we have been told, taught, and believed, could we handle it? We can't all be right, can we? Ok, you can take your deep-thinking hat off now. Fun stuff to ponder every so often, and I am very grateful for the educators I had the honor to learn under back in college.

The Back Nine

At age 54, I am on the back nine of my life, assuming I live to age 100. The front nine wasn't so bad; however, I know I can improve my game; we all can, and we must. I am very excited for the future and look forward to getting Choices Network, Ltd. off and running to do my part in raising awareness for substance abuse and addiction and, of course, to honor Seth. October 4th, 2016 now seems so long ago, yet that day will forever be embedded in the fabric of who we are.

I got my first tattoo this year and am working on my second. I hear they can become addictive - in a good way. I had it commissioned by Nate Renner, the son of my best friend and business partner, Brock Renner. Nate was 15 when he designed my tattoo. Roman and Nate are both juniors at Prairie. The Renner's have been there all along on our journey and knew Seth very well. I thought this would be a great tribute making it more personal to me.

Nate's Original Artwork (Left) and Me Getting My Tattoo (Right)

It's the symbol for **living in the moment.** It has the Roman numerals (for Roman), of Seth's date of death (10/4/16) with a golf ball (for Ian) representing the middle raindrop. It's the color blue to signify the love for scuba diving Roman and I share. We have been to Cozumel and Bonaire over the past 12 months trying to live life for us and in honor of Seth. We have a trip to Roatan scheduled for later this year.

Bonaire Scuba Trip December 2019

As I wrap up writing this book, we are experiencing a global disruption that has so far wreaked havoc on the markets, jobs, and the psyche of the entire planet. We are amid a global pandemic going by the name of COVID-19 (the novel Coronavirus). At the grocery stores recently, more people were in the beer and wine department than anywhere else. Reports for March 2020 showed a 53% jump in alcohol sales compared to the same time last year. According to new data being released by the CDC, drug overdoses killed nearly 72,000 Americans in 2019, a record high. 2020 is on track to be even worse during the pandemic.

COVID-19 will not be the last inducer of stress and anxiety; I am sure of that. I also know that alcohol and drugs have **NEVER** been the answer to deal with these issues and concerns, and **NEVER** will be. Unfortunately, I believe as we look back at the data in a few years, we will see a tremendous spike in depression, substance abuse, divorce, and possibly suicide from the pressures this has and will cause.

I know many younger people are looking at this as apocalyptic - coupled with the 2008 global recession, the 2001 tech bubble, and 9/11 being during their lifetime. They feel they have been dealt a harsh card in life over the past almost 20 years. Yes, they have, but by no means is this something our country and humanity hasn't endured in the past. If you take someone born in 1864 and dying in 1943 (79 years old) would have lived in their lifetime:

The Civil War
World War I
Cholera
The Spanish Flu (25-50 million died worldwide)
The Great Depression
Measles and Polio
The Holocaust
World War II

Just to put things in perspective. We are strong, and we will become stronger after this, even as we inevitably move on to the next crisis.

The universe is under no obligation to make sense to us or owe us anything in return. We can only and should only focus on what we can do daily to improve ourselves in a manner consistent with the overall compatibility with nature and others. Refer to the Ten Principles previously discussed as a refresher if needed.

The illusion of the self is an intriguing proposition that I have recently begun to explore. The "I" and "me" narratives in our experiences and the perceptions we all have, help to form the quality of our interactions with others. I plan on delving into this as well as the tangled concept of free will as I navigate the back nine of my life. I have alluded to the continued focus on breaking down the barriers we self-impose, to be willing to listen to reason, and to keep learning. Maybe another book will work its way out of my head?

Part of my journey is advancing the idea that most challenges and obstacles can, with practice, be dealt with in a constructive manner. Anger, regret, greed, fear, and envy are exhaustive human emotions that distract us from where our attention is needed most. In the short term, they may provide an impetus for creativity and motivation, yet long term, they are very destructive. They slowly suck away the positive energy we have like emotional vampires draining us of our strength and optimism. Just like alcohol, drugs and substance abuse does to the afflicted. Learning coping mechanisms to combat the stresses of life will undoubtedly help those prone to substance abuse and addictions.

I hope after reading this book, it's plausible for you to see there are other ways to look at life's events when they happen. Knowing and expecting them to happen is half the battle. Faith doesn't have the same interpretation for everyone. Tremendous good can come out of horrendous bad. It must. **Deny permitting substance abuse and addictions the benefit of entering your extraordinary life and when they do find healthy ways to engage and contest them.** They are not allowed anymore. There are always two roads you can travel. I implore you to use your pain and suffering to become a beacon to guide you on your unique path to healing.

"Everything can be taken from a man but one thing:
The last of the human freedoms - to choose one's attitude
in any given set of circumstances, to choose one's own
way."
-Viktor Frankl

I would like to submit a few things I have learned over my lifetime that were reinforced after Seth's death. Thoughts or steps for those in battle with substance abuse, addiction, and mental health: **You are not alone!**

MY 12 DAILY STEPS:

1. **Win** the day — nothing more, nothing less.
2. You can't undo your addiction, embrace it. It's part of **your story** but will not negatively define you.
3. You don't get over trauma. It's part of **your story** but will not negatively define you.
4. Addictions need not be negative. Be addicted to telling the **truth,** your **health,** and **your family.**
5. You can always tell yourself a **new story** about your past.
6. **Meditate, read, laugh, and cry** daily.
7. Have goals but not at the expense of **living in the moment.**
8. Never waste a **good failure.**
9. We all suffer. We all die. We all can be happy. One of these **isn't a choice.**
10. **Attention** redeems most anything in the moment.
11. You're not a label. You're a **miracle.**
12. Live your life **UNDETERRED.**

In February of this year (2020) Roman penned a song he likes to play on his ukulele as a tribute to Seth, it's called "Open Book":

OPEN BOOK (Seth's Song)

I just wanna spend more moments with you,
but I know that can't come true.
We wrote a book together and in the end,
All that was missing was just you.

I went through heaven and hell to look for you,
But I didn't even have to move.
That little book we wrote is called Life,
And there still is so much more to write, cause

All life is an open book, we can write pages and let people
look at our stories and adventures that we've all gone on,
even when some of us are already gone. Some are gone,
including the ones we held very close to our hearts.

I just want to say one last goodbye, so please don't go off
and cry.

We can all remember that day, the day you went away, but
that doesn't mean we can't smile, knowing that you'll come

and stay awhile.

We have to start looking at Life with all the pages we can write, cause

All Life is is an open book, we can write chapters and let people look at our actions and consequences that we all made, even ones that happened to be a mistake.

These aren't mistakes, all we made were the chapters and the story, the friends and family, the hearts, and the lives that we changed."
- Roman Johnston 2020

Roman with his Ukulele

I sincerely want to thank you for taking the time to join me in telling our story. Walking side by side with us should give you a fresh new perspective on your life. Seth was a wonderful person that made some very poor choices as he grew older and paid the ultimate price. I have no doubt he would have made a great dad. My relationship with Seth didn't end with his death; instead, I feel it's just reborn. I feel as if I know him better now than I ever did when he was alive. I live inspired by Seth and am so fortunate to have known him. Although it wasn't as long as I would have wished, he made me into the man I am today, and for that, I am working very hard to pay him back. **I owe him nothing less.** I cry every single day, but the tears themselves have evolved and don't carry the weight of suffering and sorrow as they once did. They now flow with hope, optimism, and courage. I am sure that's what Seth would have wanted for all of us.

I hinted in the introduction that after reading this book, you would discover my motivation, my inspiration, and my ultimate goal for this endeavor. Better yet, I hoped you would find something in my story that resonated with you, which would help you gain new awareness, insight, or perspective in your own life. I have faith I was right.

This could easily have become a sad, depressing story, but with the help of so many wonderful people, we are turning a corner, and the opportunities in front of us are endless. We have a tremendous amount of work and growth ahead of us, yet we enthusiastically anticipate the many new relationships we will embrace in this next stage of our lives. Take the time to tell those you care about that you **love** them. Right now, at this moment, not tomorrow. In my introduction, I asked a simple question to you.

I will close with the same question: *The results of life's final exam will be revealed long after your death, and in the legacy you leave. What will your legacy be?*

Young Seth Playing Football

One of Seth's Early School Photos

Young Seth Learning to Ride A Bike
He Was Not Very Happy About The Helmet!

Me with Roman, Seth and Ian

Seth's Basketball Photo

233

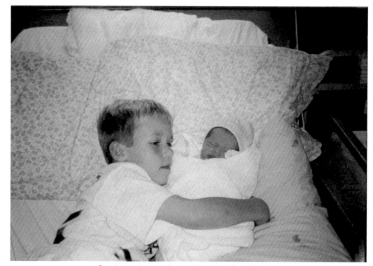

Seth with newborn Ian in May 2001

Me and Seth in Hilton Head, SC

Ian, Seth & Roman

Seth Before The First Day of School

Seth

Seth and I in Chicago for the Big 10 Tournament

Special Acknowledgement

This project being my first real attempt at a book I went into this quite unprepared. As I humbly stumbled through writing on a yellow pad of paper, I eventually evolved to Google Docs (new concept to me). Along this journey I learned much and am very appreciative of all the wonderful people who have assisted me. There is one person whom I am extremely grateful for and I am sure for whom they are pleased to see me complete this project so they may have their life back! Molly Nordlocken has been instrumental to me in not only preparing for, "This One's For You" but all the odd technological requests I have given to her over the years.

She has worked tirelessly to assemble all the videos, news reports and pictures of Ian's golf career for me personally and for this book. She has helped with submitting applications and nominations for Ian's various awards. Many times, as I wept in her presence, she provided an open space for me to let my emotions out, without judgement. Often in life you meet people who are simply genuine and caring. This is Molly. For all the last-minute frantic calls at midnight and early weekend morning texts she has never complained. Well, there was this one time......:)

Molly has been giving back to the community for years. She has been instrumental in organizing our team for the annual Walk for Alzheimer's in Cedar Rapids and also is an active board member of the Linn County TRIAD, an organization assisting and providing resources to senior citizens. Lastly, I was proud to ask her to be a board member of my Non-Profit, The Choices Network, Ltd. She is a member of the inaugural board of directors consisting of Kenyon Murray, Douglas Wagner, Daniel Walterman and of course, our Youth Ambassador, Roman Johnston. Molly, without you this book does not happen. It's as simple as that. Thank you for being you and challenging me along the way!

Jeff Johnston

Acknowledgements

Whether you are a stranger I met on the golf course, someone I specifically mention in the book, or a member of my close inner circle, I want to express my sincere appreciation for everyone who has been a part of our story so far. Although this journey has no ending, it is important to continue the conversations around addiction and mental health. Thank you for allowing me to share our story and honor Seth's memory.

Additional Resources

For additional resources and links to things
mentioned in the book, visit:

www.ThisOnesForYouBook.com

CHOICES NETWORK, LTD.

Help Us Continue Seth's Story

www.TheChoicesNetwork.org